MINISTRIES THROUGH
NON-PARISH INSTITUTIONS

Into Our Third Century Series

MINISTRIES THROUGH NON-PARISH INSTITUTIONS

William E. Ramsden

Ezra Earl Jones, Editor

ABINGDON   Nashville

MINISTRIES THROUGH NON-PARISH INSTITUTIONS

Library of Congress Cataloging in Publication Data

RAMSDEN, WILLIAM E. 1932-
Ministries through non-parish institutions.
(Into our third century)
Includes bibliographical references.
1. Church work—United Methodist Church (United
States)
I. Title. II. Series.
BX8382.2.R35   259   80-22294

ISBN 0-687-27037-5

MANUFACTURED BY THE PARTHENON PRESS AT
NASHVILLE, TENNESSEE, UNITED STATES OF AMERICA

Contents

Foreword

In 1984 United Methodism will observe the 200th anniversary of the Christmas Conference of 1784—the date most often regarded as the beginning of the Methodist movement in the United States. We shall pause to remember how the Wesleyan vision of holy love and active piety spread like an unquenchable flame as the United States expanded from coast to coast; how people of all races, cultures, and classes rallied to a gospel offering salvation and demanding good works as the fruit of Christian faith in God.

But we shall do more. Our bicentennial is also a time to soberly anticipate the future, to take stock of ourselves as we move into our third century. Our inheritance is rich in faith and works. It nourishes us but our tasks are now, and tomorrow. The United Methodist Church is large (9.6 million members in the United States), still highly visible and active, but some indicators of our future prospects are disturbing. We shall reflect on and discuss these concerns as United Methodists until we once again catch a vision of ministry and service that is worthy of our past, builds upon our present, and thrusts us again into the mainstream of human life with the message of God's redeeming love.

You, a United Methodist lay member or pastor, and your congregation have a vital role in both the celebration and the search. It is the people in the pews and pulpits of United Methodism who must reestablish our identity and purpose through discussion on who we are as United Methodists, what we wish to accomplish, and how we pursue our goals in the years ahead.

Into Our Third Century, initiated by the General Council on Ministries with the encouragement of the Council of Bishops, is intended to support your efforts. Over a four-year period, beginning in 1980, eighteen separate volumes are being released for your use. The present book *Ministries Through Non-Parish Institutions* is the sixth volume in the series. Other books scheduled for release in coming months will deal with outreach ministry, social movements and issues, church leadership and management, ecumenical relationships, ethnic minority constituencies, understanding faith, professional ministry, general agencies, financial support, and polity.

The current volume by William Ramsden focuses on the long-standing relationship between The United Methodist Church and schools, colleges, hospitals, retirement homes, children's residences, community centers, and other forms of non-parish institutions. Dr. Ramsden discusses how these relationships developed over two centuries, the purposes of the church in extending its ministry through these institutions, the ability of the institutions to adapt their services as social conditions have changed, the present tenuous situations of many of these organizations, and assesses alternatives for future ministry by The United Methodist Church through non-parish institutions. We think you will be both enlightened and inspired. Your response will also be welcomed by the members and staff of the Council.

Norman E. Dewire
General Secretary

Ezra Earl Jones
Editor

The General Council on Ministries
601 West Riverview Avenue
Dayton, Ohio 45406

February, 1981

CHAPTER 1

Introduction

What's This All About?

"We have a lot of money tied up in institutions. Is that the best way for us to be in mission?"

"I read that colleges are going to be faced with declining enrollment this decade. Does that mean we will have to provide extra financial support for our colleges?"

"We have a finger in so many pies with so many different agencies doing so many different things that it's hard to know just what we *are* doing, let alone whether that is what we ought to be doing."

"There are agencies in our conference that have been at work for years while I have been a member of the conference, but I still don't really know anything about what they do or why we're related to them."

"It's sinful the way that Pacific Homes mess is using up so much money for legal fees that ought to be going into mission. Could that happen here?"

"Whose business is it to keep in touch with all those institutions anyway?"

"How in the world did we United Methodists ever get such a bewildering array of special organizations doing so many things?"

Such questions of United Methodist leaders are matched by others that leaders in institutions have been asking:

"I see The United Methodist Church in a period of shrinkage in the money it has available to fund institutions like ours. What is that going to mean for our relationship?"

"Does anybody in the church really understand what we are trying to do and why? Does anybody really care?"

"Will fear of more Pacific Homes situations cause the church to pull back in its relationship to us?"

"We've always been 'United Methodist related,' but sometimes I wonder whether that really means anything."

"There are so many channels of responsibility that we have in our community, such as the various levels of government and their regulatory agencies. Can we still be church-related while meeting all those other requirements so necessary to our very operation?"

All these questions deal with the relationship between The United Methodist Church and a vast range of institutions (hospitals, homes, schools, etc.) that are labeled in a variety of ways, all meaning at least "United Methodist-related." The time has come when such questions must be faced. United Methodism is confronted with too many challenges to allow traditional relationships to "bump along" while the capacity of the church to respond through its institutions and to support them is eroded. This book is intended to help United Methodists to understand better what their church-related institutions are about, what the basic issues are, and what some options for response may be. We will seek answers to fundamental questions:

> How did we get all those institutions?
> What are they doing for us?
> Why should we be concerned now?
> Do we really need all those institutions?
> Should we still be related? If so, how?
> What can we expect next?
> Where do we go from here?

One chapter is devoted to each of these questions. But first there are three other questions that need answering. Why should I bother to try to understand all of this? Just what is a "non-parish institution"? What is this study?

Why Bother? Why This Study?

You don't need to be a conference official responsible for relating to one or more church-related institutions to have a stake in the issues surrounding those relationships. It is often the activity of an institution identified as United Methodist that produces the questions or comments that friends, neighbors, and coworkers direct to United Methodists about their church. The litigation resulting from the bankruptcy of United Methodist related Pacific Homes produced in 1979 unfavorable national media treatment of the denomination on TV's "Sixty Minutes" and in the *Wall Street Journal*. This situation is the most dramatic, but all along many have been asking questions about the church's relation to institutions. You may need to be informed just to be able to invite a friend to consider visiting or joining your church.

Further, the "fallout" from Pacific Homes has been landing on United Methodist boards and conferences as well. Many are questioning whether they should continue to be related to various institutions if one outcome could be a crippling lawsuit (and as the Pacific and Southwest Conference has learned, the crippling effect begins with the negative publicity and the costs of litigation). Such issues usually provoke controversy and lead to working out decisions through United Methodist political processes—formal debate in Annual Conference (or other forums), and the informal discussions, personal contacts, etc. that precede and surround it. Those political forums work best in deciding contentious issues when those debating and voting have a clear sense of the informed concerns of their members. You can contribute directly or indirectly to that process just by being informed.

Since the fundamental purpose of non-parish institutions is to extend the mission of the local church, local churches can benefit from as well as contribute to the relationship. However, both finding the means to support an extended mission and developing ways to gain insight and inspiration from it will be more effective when basic issues are understood. This book will consider what kinds of support are the best for the immediate future and analyze the overall situation to help churches discover ways to build relationships through which they can learn and grow.

What Is a Non-Parish Institution?

While there are many kinds of institutions related to The United Methodist Church, from the church's perspective they all share a basic purpose and three central characteristics. That purpose can be summarized as extending the ministry and mission of The United Methodist Church. Each non-parish institution shares with all other United Methodist mission ventures the task of meeting needs that are beyond the scope of the local church and/or require a special organization. Each also represents a judgment that the best way to meet certain needs is through an independent institution rather than through a local church, district, conference, or national agency.

The first basic characteristic that follows directly from that purpose is the institution's focus on meeting some cluster of human needs. Hospitals meet health care needs, schools meet needs for education, community centers meet needs for social service and community development, and so on. The needs addressed are rarely involved directly with evangelism but represent a contemporary expression of Jesus' healing ministry and such teachings as the parable of the last judgment in which the "sheep and goats" are distinguished by their response to elementary human needs, such as food, drink, shelter, and companionship. The point was made clearly by a conference United Methodist Women's president when she responded to a question on the mission she saw a particular agency performing on behalf of United Methodism: "Does this mean 'supporting United Methodism?' If so, I'm offended at the emphasis. The important part is people's lives being changed."

A second basic characteristic of these institutions is their functional autonomy. Each is to a considerable degree able to make decisions on its policies and activities without having to get permission from The United Methodist Church. Some of these institutions are actually owned by and nominally operated by a United Methodist body. Others have some portion of their board elected by one or more Annual Conferences. Many operate within policies that have been approved by (or at least cleared with) an Annual Conference or one of its boards or by a national board. Even in those cases, however, the daily operation of the agency is in the hands of its staff, with ongoing accountability to its own board of trustees or board of directors. They are "non-parish" institutions because they are not directly related to any single congregation; they are "institutions" because they have functional autonomy to direct their own operations (perhaps within some broad limits outlined by some responsibility to a United Methodist body).

On the other hand, a third characteristic is that all such institutions stand in an acknowledged relationship to United Methodism. Sometimes there are formal statements in charters and by laws specifying a United Methodist connection. Often there is a name incorporating the denomination's name or one from its tradition (e.g., Wesley or Otterbein). Almost always there is a connection with at least one beyond-the-local-church United Methodist body, usually a conference board or committee, a unit of a national board, or the United Methodist Women. How much the relationship is publicized by either the church or the institution varies greatly, but almost always some fact of relationship is proclaimed, or at least admitted, and is embodied in a specific connection between church body and institution.

Another way of understanding what non-parish institutions are is to look at the variety of institutions that are actually related to The United Methodist Church. When the General Council on Ministries convened a task force of program board staff to define some of the problems involved, they identified over two dozen types of non-parish institutions, placing them in four basic groups:

Health Care Institutions

General Hospitals
Children's Hospitals
Clinics
Health Care Centers

Nursing Homes and other
  Palliative Care
Psychological Centers

Homes

Retirement
Children's
Youth
Foster

Residence Halls
Transition and "Halfway
  Houses
Low Cost Housing Projects

Schools

Preschool
Elementary
Secondary
Mission
Colleges

Universities
Seminaries
Campus Ministries
Wesley Foundations

Community Centers—Rural and Urban

Counseling
Community Development
Recreation
Child Care/Day Care
Food/Clothing

Senior Citizen Services:
  Meals-on-Wheels
  Transportation
  Legal

You may be able to think of special institutions which fit these types. If you can confidently name one that is United Methodist related for each major grouping you are probably more knowledgeable than most people.

What Is This Study?

This book is based primarily on a survey of persons related to a sampling of institutions and of United Methodists in the conferences in which those institutions are located. All were asked how they perceived the specific agency and its relationship to United Methodism.

Since it would have been an overwhelming task to cover all institutions or even all types of institutions, we chose six types of agencies, drew a small sample of institutions in each type, and then interviewed a few persons about each institution. The six types which seemed common were finally represented by ten hospitals, fifteen colleges, nine retirement residences, and eight mission agencies of miscellaneous function for a total of sixty-three institutions.

The sample for each type of institution was drawn with the help of staff in the appropriate divisions of various boards. The chief administrators of those agencies were then contacted by telephone to determine if they were willing to have their agency included in the study. When that cooperation was secured, further contacts were made to provide a combination of questionnaire- and telephone-interview responses from related persons. The chief administrator (or designated representative) and the chairperson of the board (or another active board member), and a program staffperson were sought for each. For hospitals, two staff were contacted, a physician (Chief of Medical Service) and a nurse (Chief of Nursing Service). Similarly, a faculty member in the area of religion or the humanities and a faculty member in one of the science departments were contacted for each college.

Members of the General Council on Ministries suggested clergy and laypersons in the Annual Conferences in which the institutions were located, and those persons were asked to complete matching questionnaires and to respond to a telephone interview. In order to get a spread of perceptions, one person in each of four categories was asked to respond for each institution: the chairperson of the conference board to which that institution would usually relate, the conference president of United Methodist Women, a knowledgeable local church pastor, and an active layman.

When the returns were closed to process the data, 274 questionnaires and 378 interview reports were on hand.

The dimensions to be investigated and the questions for the questionnaires and interviews were prepared in three stages. (1) Analyses and possible questions were developed for each type of agency through consulting the literature of the various disciplines involved and calling on expert consultants in the areas of higher education, health care, and social service. (2) Site visits and face-to-face interviews with persons in each type of agency tested potential questions. (3) Questionnaire and interview forms were established. Questionnaire forms had matching questions to permit direct comparison among the various types of institutions. They were used to provide numerical data that could be analyzed statistically. Interview schedules were more differentiated than the questionnaires, but still comparable. They opened opportunity for nuances of feeling and perception to be voiced.

Acknowledgments

While the author is responsible for the data and its interpretation in this volume, the cooperation and efforts of many others contributed to the implementation of the study. Staff members of general boards helped build the sample and shared their concerns. The staff of the Division of Higher Education of the Board of Higher Education and Ministry, and the Health and Welfare Ministries Division and the National Division of the Board of Global Ministries were particularly helpful. Members of the General Council on Ministries helped identify contact persons in the Annual Conferences. Three hundred seventy-eight persons in institutions and conferences provided information.

Special thanks must also go to Amy V'Ancona, Lucy Pierre, and Bradley Sheeks for conducting telephone interviews; to Diane Carlson for handling data processing; and to David Brown for typing and mailing questionnaires, and typing drafts of this manuscript. Four persons provided special expertise in the content areas related to the institutional survey—advising on dimensions to be studied and on interpretation of data—Louise Shoemaker and Richard Estes, Dean and Director of Research, respectively, at the School of Social Work of the University of Pennsylvania; William Kissick, Professor of Research Medicine and Health Care System, School of Medicine, University of Pennsylvania; and Malcolm Warford, Advisor to the President and Professor of Religion and Education, Union Theological Seminary. Edith Goodwin gave leadership to the design of the study on behalf of the General Council on Ministries staff and Ezra Earl Jones performed beautifully the central task of editor, comforting and confronting as needed.

CHAPTER 2

How Did We Get
All Those Institutions?

While the variety is bewildering and the present connections sometimes seem tenuous, each institution related to The United Methodist Church had its origins in recognition by United Methodists of needs they felt had a just claim on their Christian response, followed by determination to do something about those needs. Such determination has usually led to programs in local churches, in Annual Conferences, and in other United Methodist bodies. However, sometimes the desire to respond to the need has created an institution.

Some institutional responses were based on existing models. For instance, United Methodists saw colleges providing higher education, so they assumed that the way to meet that need in their community was to start a college. Or, they knew hospitals cared for the sick and so channeled their concern for caring for the sick and dying into the creation of a hospital in their community.

In other cases, the institution evolved from a program of a United Methodist board or agency. The original committee providing oversight for a project was transformed into the board of directors when acquisition of property led to the formation of an independent corporation to manage and hold it.

In several instances an institution was first brought into existence under other auspices, and United Methodists later became its sponsors. Even in these instances, the key judgments seem to have been that the institution was needed and that it would do that task better under United Methodist auspices.

The reality underlying these developments is twofold. Complex needs take concentrated attention, and the more complex the needs are the more concentration is required. Thus, an organization with a special focus on those needs tends to appear. Similarly, enduring needs must be met through an ongoing response; and responses that outlive the persons who start them need some social body in which to incarnate the continuing concern. An institution provides just such a social body.

The organic image of a body is especially appropriate to these institutions; they change, they grow, they die. In fact, their whole history can be read as a series of institutional adaptations to changing needs and conditions. No agency existing for more than a few years preserves intact its initial definition of mission, methods, and organization. Radical changes occur, ranging from sudden major shifts in function to mergers of different institutions into new ones. However, most adaptations come in small steps, and it is only with the perspective of time that the sweeping nature of the resulting change can be seen. Characteristic profiles of the history of some types of institutions and samples of typical histories of particular agencies reveal this process better than abstract definition. (In preparation for this survey, histories were taken from files or publications of national boards. However, none of the institutions whose histories are given were included in the survey sample.)

Colleges

As the church moved West with the expanding frontier, one early need it found in growing communities was education. United Methodism responded to that need by creating or assisting in creating schools. When the frontier time had passed, and the communities were becoming more settled in their growth, the educational concern shifted to higher education. Again, United Methodism was responsive. Concerns for training clergy and laypersons able to lead in church and community together with concern to provide a Christian environment for higher learning led to the establishment of colleges. Some existing schools simply extended their focus of education into the college years. In other cases new colleges were formed.

By the latter half of the nineteenth century, United Methodists were adapting to a new situation. Civic pride in growing communities often sought expression through the creation of a college. There was strong community sentiment and leadership for the creation of a college, and there was The United Methodist Church, well-established in the town, willing and able to assist in the development of colleges, and a guarantor of the stability and rectitude of a new school beyond the geographical scope and lifetime of its founders.

Thus, the process of adaptation was already present at the beginning for many colleges. That adaptation continued thereafter, leading many colleges into mergers, new curricula, expansion, and sometimes dissolution. High schools became junior colleges, which then became four-year colleges. Colleges added professional schools or seminaries added other professional schools and a liberal arts college to become universities.

Two examples of such evolution can be found in Albright College and Nebraska Wesleyan University. Albright College's beginnings were threefold. The Evangelical Association started Union Seminary in New Berlin, Pennsylvania, changing its name and its function in 1887 to Central Pennsylvania College. Meanwhile, the East Pennsylvania Conference of the Evangelical Association had started Schuylkill College in Reading, Pennsylvania, in 1881. In 1886, it moved to Fredericksburg, but moved back to Reading in 1902. The Evangelical Association also started the Albright Collegiate Institute in Myerstown, Pennsylvania, in 1895. In 1902, Albright Collegiate Institute and Central Pennsylvania College merged to become Albright College (in Myerstown).

Finally, in 1928, Albright College and Schuylkill College merged to become Albright College in Reading—the present institution. With denomination mergers it became an Evangelical United Brethren college in 1946 and a United Methodist school in 1966.

Nebraska Wesleyan's history begins with a predecessor institution, Cass County University, which operated only from 1853 to 1856. About thirty years later, Nebraska Methodists showed a burst of energy in forming colleges: York Seminary was begun in 1879; 1884 saw the creation of Nebraska Central College by the North Nebraska Conference (in York) and North Central Methodist College was begun in Central City (and later moved to Fullerton); in 1886, Mallalieu University was started by West Nebraska Conference (in Bartley) and Orleans College was begun in Orleans. The very next year saw two sets of mergers. First, Nebraska Central, Mallalieu, and Orleans merged to start Nebraska Wesleyan University. Then, York Seminary and North Central Methodist merged with it and the institution moved to Lincoln, finishing the process of creation. Instruction began in 1888. Finally, in 1940, the school was reorganized as a liberal arts college. Its affiliation shifted with denominational mergers, from Methodist Episcopal to Methodist to United Methodist.

Health and Welfare Institutions

While colleges represented predominantly a response to the pressing needs of rural America for education, health and welfare institutions began primarily as a response to the needs of urban America. Children without parents or homes needed care, so orphanages were developed. Youth, children, and families were being submerged by industrialization and slum conditions in big cities. Settlement houses in their various forms were created. The poor were frequently the sick, and the desire to respond to that need with health care produced hospitals.

As times changed, the institutions changed. The orphanages

became "homes," they began to include foster care, and gradually began to focus on intensive care for the minority of children and youth needing that level of attention. The settlement houses became community centers (with the shift in philosophy the name change symbolizes, changing from something sent in to something trying to be indigenous). More recently, another wave of adaptation has spread through the centers leading to a dispersion of activities and an emphasis on advocacy empowerment of community people. Hospitals responded to the waves of changes moving through health care and were picked up and carried on the stream of that evolution. Increasingly, their distinctiveness as United Methodist was felt in terms of tradition and desire to maintain relationship and to respond to value of humane treatment. The basic features of the hospitals were shaped by the changes in the field; for instance, research and education emphases, technology of greater power and higher cost, dependence on third-party payment contracts (insurance and government programs, e.g., Medicaid).

The richness of this history becomes manifest in the stories of individual institutions. New England Deaconess Hospital began as a project of the Methodist Deaconesses at the New England Deaconess Home and Training School in Boston. In 1896, they opened a brownstone house as a fourteen-bed home-hospital as a part of their service to the poor and sick of the city. In 1898, they graduated their first class of deaconess nurses (one of whom became hospital administrator from 1901 to 1924). The policy was to serve all people, and records show that in the first four years a total of 658 patients represented 23 nationalities, 16 denominations, and 68 occupations. Also, in 1899, the nursing school reorganized to give a standard professional course and began admitting students who were not deaconesses. In 1907 the hospital moved to a new fifty-bed facility, beginning a twentieth-century record of steady expansion. Early concentrations to meet special community needs included care of the terminally ill and of diabetes sufferers. These pacesetters established the hospital's trend toward specialization and research (with the terminal illness concern leading to a focus on cancer research). In its early years, the hospital was a part of the New England Deaconess Association, which operated a number of social service institutions, but in 1929, the hospital became a separate corporation. At that same time, a physician became superintendent, symbolically marking the fact that control and allegiance had passed from deaconess outreach to medical service. In fact, a 1971 hospital publication devotes thirty-one pages to the history of the hospital, and the word Methodist appears only three times, twice in identifying the denominational affiliation of the deaconesses and once as part of the name of another institution in the New England Deaconess Association.

Conversely, Methodist Hospital of Lubbuck, Texas, began in 1917 as a proprietary hospital. Then Lubbock Sanitarium, it was owned and operated by a small group of physicians. It served a general hospital function, and as it grew, its name was eventually changed to Lubbock General Hospital (in 1941). In 1945, ownership was transferred to a nonprofit foundation created by the hospital's physician-owners. Expansion had been occurring, so a major move was made to a suburban location and a new $3.5 million building in 1953. Within six months a special session of the Northwest Texas Conference had assumed ownership of the hospital, changing its name to Methodist Hospital. Expansion of services and facilities have characterized the hospital since then—as has a giant United Methodist emblem on its exterior. Bed capacity has increased to over five hundred, modern treatment methods and technology have been secured, a new chapel has been built, and the Chaplains' Department has grown to two chaplains and a full clinical pastoral education program.

The Methodist Home of Macon, Georgia, began its existence in 1852 as a county "Widows' and Orphans' Asylum." By 1872, the county found the expenses too much for its taxpayers, so the operation was sold for one dollar to the South

Georgia Conference of the Methodist Episcopal Church, South. Methodist stewardship raised the money to replace the original building when it burned, and to add new buildings over time, as well as to underwrite the expenses of service. Residential services were primary, with placement in private homes secondary in the early decades. The peak number of residents occurred in 1915. By 1940, functions had changed so much that the name of the home was changed from The Orphans Home of the South Georgia Conference to The Methodist Home. At the same time it received its first license from the State Department of Welfare and affiliated with the General Board of Hospitals and Homes (now the Health and Welfare Division of the Board of Global Ministries). The emphasis on treatment continued to develop so that after 1960, the proportion of children in residence at any one time to the total number of children served declined steadily.

The roots of the Indiana United Methodist Children's Home are in the action of a deaconess in providing a home for two neglected little girls in 1915. Quickly, with the help of interested friends, the home was endorsed by the Indiana Conference. In 1922, the Conference took over ownership and management of the home, with Northwest Indiana Conference joining a year later. Started in Greencastle, the home was moved to Lebanon in 1924; and the years from then on are a record of expanding facilities. The shifting philosophy in recent years is revealed in five events. The first professionally-educated psychiatric social worker was employed in 1959, beginning the transition from a custodial type of home to a residential treatment center for emotionally disturbed children. In 1964, the first executive director with professional social work training was hired. In 1965 the state licensed the home for child placement, beginning its foster home program. In the following half-decade, five group homes were opened in various parts of the state. Then, in 1972, the first lay president of the Board of Trustees was elected.

Wesley House Community Center of Meridian, Mississippi, also began with the concern of a dedicated few. Two Methodist women determined to make the church real for poor families in a cottonmill town on Meridian's boundary. They began a school program in 1904, with day classes for children and evening classes for adults. Cooking and sewing classes were offered to women. By 1906 they had become the City Mission Board. Surviving destruction by tornado of their building, they enlisted their first city missionary and added a free medical clinic in 1910. Rapid growth brought a deaconess from the Home Mission Board of the Methodist Episcopal Church, South. Services continued, varying their emphases by the needs most manifest and by the skills volunteers or workers could bring to the home. Expansions of facility occurred again in 1927 and 1966, and just recently a new building has replaced the old one, with contributions from many individuals and business firms. In it, six staff and seventy-five volunteers (in an average month) continue the tradition of meeting community needs.

The Marcy-Newberry Association of Chicago illustrates the principal of response to changing communities and the initiative of United Methodist Women. The work began under the impetus of the Rock River Conference Women's Home Missionary Society and the City Missionary Society in 1883, with the intention of ministering to Bohemian immigrants. By 1896, the national society provided money for a new building and the Elizabeth Marcy Home was opened (named after its promoter and chairperson). Before long, the population of the neighborhood was changing, with Jewish immigrants becoming predominant. The Home shifted focus to become a center of training and support for adjustment to the United States and for Christian concern for Jewish persons. When the Jewish population began moving to a community to the west, Marcy Home moved with them, opening its new building in 1930 in the Lawndale section of Chicago. The Home Missionary Society determined to keep the old location open to serve persons moving in around it. During the 1930s its work was primarily with Mexican-Americans and secondarily with the black people beginning to move into the district. During the postwar years, the neighborhoods of both Marcy Center and Newberry Center (the new name for the old location on Newberry Avenue) became predominantly black. Newberry was surrounded by new public housing projects and a new elementary school. The programs at each adapted to the changing needs, and as their services became more similarly focused, the two centers joined into one association. A new building was built at Newberry in the mid-1960s, but the property (and concern for its upkeep) has followed from the old Home Missionary Society to its present successor, the Women's Division of the Board of Global Ministries.

In addition to the expanding frontier with its rural needs and the burgeoning cities with their urban needs, one other nineteenth century social movement elicited a major United Methodist institutional response. The freeing of black slaves raised many problems for black persons who had not been prepared by their work. The northern Methodists were among the most active groups in establishing training schools for adults (job and homemaking skills) and schools and colleges for young people. Many of these institutions have evolved into colleges, community centers, and hospitals in the present galaxy of United Methodist-related institutions.

Indeed, it was the passionate concern of Elizabeth L. Rust that led directly to creation of the Women's Home Missionary Society. She had been roused by a visit with her minister husband to friends in New Orleans in 1876. She met two women who were trying to reach out in ministry to the needs of freed black women. While the focus of the Society broadened quickly to include a wide range of needs and projects, one of its primary interests for years remained with its projects for black people. This outreach at first ran from women of the church in the North to projects in the South, but before long began to look to similar programs in northern cities.

Residences

Two types of institutions that varied from the community service pattern in origin are retirement residences and women's residences. Both were initially intended to provide a service for United Methodists—the one for older persons needing protected and supportive living environments and the other for young women moving to the city to work. Both types have undergone great change.

The women's residences have been confronted by the need for radical shifts in philosophy as the need for their past services has disappeared. A variety of changes in property use have occurred. A particularly imaginative reuse involves providing a home for persons leaving mental institutions, drug and alcohol treatment centers, prisons, etc., to help them adjust to life in the outside and to build and refine their skills for coping legally and effectively with life. Here, the function of residence is continued as is the concept of meeting needs during transition, but the transition involved has changed drastically. The service purpose has shifted entirely to focus on community needs, not on those of young United Methodist women.

The first big breakthrough in retirement residences was the shift to fees paid by residents as the major income source. The second came through the possibilities opened up by federally guaranteed and interest-rate-subsidized loans for construction. The net result of these changes has been to make retirement residences much more oriented to community service, in part because the conditions attached to federal loans make it illegal to discriminate by religion in accepting residents. The history of two retirement homes demonstrates this process.

The United Methodist Homes of New Jersey began with a simple home and six residents in Ocean Grove. It aimed to provide an alternative for older persons to the county poorhouse if they could not live with family. In 1916 the home became affiliated with both Methodist conferences in the state, and the following year's conference reports began showing contributions from churches to the Home. Capacity rose to twenty in 1910, and after a fire in 1916, the new building accommodated fifty (raised to ninety-two by 1922). The next major expansion came in 1949, with a new building, having a capacity of 230, built to meet newly emerging needs and concepts of housing and services for the elderly, using the new federal funding programs. The next round of expansion followed a decision to decentralize, and from 1959 to 1974, six additional homes were constructed in various parts of the state. Through all these years active auxiliaries have provided connections between the homes and the local churches of the conferences. More recent expansion has been tending toward program rather than property, with the homes adding a mobile meals program in 1971, home visiting and education/consultation services in 1975, and a youth service program in 1977.

Frasier Meadows Manor in Boulder, Colorado, exemplifies the most frequent developmental history of retirement homes: they started as various government financial assistance programs made construction and service more feasible. The idea first came to the Colorado Conference from its Retired Ministers Association in 1949. It was 1952 before the Conference authorized formal investigation, and 1956 before property was received and a corporation created to develop a home. Construction did not begin until December 1958, but facilities for ninety-five residents were complete in 1960. By 1965, this capacity had been doubled. By then, the focus of concern was shifting to the need for nursing care facilities. Original plans had envisioned thirty beds, but by 1973 it was obvious that a separate building with a capacity of sixty was needed. It took until 1976 for the necessary regulatory and lending approvals to be secured, so the facility was not completed until 1977, by which time the home was considering the possibility of converting residential wings to nursing care for further needed expansion of that function.

Two points stand out in reading through these and many other institutional histories. One deals with the way in which an institution comes into being; the other with the consequences of their creation.

In almost every case, the key to an institution's development has been a small group of persons, usually with one dynamic and committed leader, who got a vision of a possibility and labor almost singlemindedly to bring their vision into reality. It is those persons who convince others of the need, work to bring Annual Conference and other church action, discover and enlist the persons and agencies in the community whose assistance is necessary, and bring together the resources and persons to do the legal, property, and social construction that makes up an institution. Those institutions that have survived and thrived have been able to build that original passion, vision, and responsiveness into the ongoing life of the agency—to institutionalize it.

In this process, the role of national agencies has not been to create institutions. Rather they have performed essentially two functions. (1) They have provided information, such as statistics to help people argue their case, guidance on government and other programs that can help, and news on what other groups have already done to help to enable and reinforce a new vision. (2) They have provided technical assistance on request, such as help in selecting architects, guidance on meeting requirements of various governmental and professional bodies, and clues to success learned by others who have already traveled the same road. Often this assistance has been given by enabling persons from successful agencies of the same type to consult with leaders of a new project.

While this panorama of creation and adaptation, merger and dissolution and recreation has been going on, the world has been watching United Methodist institutions (and all other kinds of institutions as well). One result of this process has been that successful models have been picked up by public institutions. Alternatively, some public agencies have sought to enter cooperative purchase-of-service agreements with church institutions rather than starting competing publicly owned facilities. As agencies multiplied, so did the need for some form of public monitoring. Thus was produced the network of governmental and professional standards and monitoring agencies to which United Methodist institutions have become accountable.

So today we have many kinds of institutions responding to many kinds of needs. A variety of patterns of relationship to United Methodism has evolved, and those patterns are intertwined with a whole series of other relationships with agency, community, and government coordinating groups, funders, and regulators.

CHAPTER 3

What Are They Doing for Us?

For almost all institutions the primary answer to this question speaks of what the institutions are doing on behalf of United Methodism. As our review of their history has shown, the principal mission focus for the institutions has been on community needs. Many do, as we shall see, provide a variety of services directly for United Methodist church bodies, but these are secondary to their work "in the world." The best way to understand this general point is to look more specifically at the mission of six types of institutions—those included in our survey.

Hospitals

The hospitals in the survey ranged from major health centers with extensive education and research components to hospitals in rural and urban "underserved" areas (i.e. communities with fewer treatment facilities and health professionals available than national standards suggest). Their primary mission is "health care," which is more precisely, caring for the sick. Treatment of persons, research, and training or education are the chief functions. Conference persons rarely reported the research and education components, but these functions were very important to persons attached to the hospitals.

The understanding of United Methodist-related hospital personnel of these basic functions does not differ from general views in the health care system on the role of hospitals.

Hospitals are specialized institutions providing treatment for persons referred by physicians—treatment that requires the intensive and/or specialized capacity of the hospital; for instance, surgery, sophisticated diagnosis, or intensive nursing care. The patient normally arrives at a hospital at the end of a series of efforts to restore health: first, his or her own self-care (often with the help of family, friends, and the corner drugstore), then a visit to the family physician, and finally referral to a specialist who suggests hospitalization. Many hospitals also provide clinics for medical care that may substitute (especially for lower income persons) for the specialist or even the family physician. Similarly, many have emergency rooms that are used by those seeking treatment for accidents and sudden attacks of illness. Of course, patients may be admitted to a hospital on referral from its own emergency room or clinics.

The teaching hospitals use the experiences of providing such treatment to train future health care workers in necessary skills. The clinical experience is coordinated with classroom and laboratory education in the hospital (and often with a neighboring college or university). The education programs range all the way from in-service training for nurses' aides to residencies preparing a physician for practice as a specialist. Also, in many cases hospitals provide the opportunity to practice under supervision, which comprises the clinical aspect of an education program that is otherwise academic. For instance, nursing, physical therapy, occupational therapy, and speech and therapy are all four-year college or university programs that include placement of students in hospitals for clinical education.

Research complements education in hospitals' efforts to serve all potential patients, by advancing the state of the art and the knowledge of its practitioners. Special laboratories for experiments with animals and even microorganisms are used both to develop new techniques of treatment and to understand better bodily and biological processes. Hospitals with mental health units and/or with special concerns for understanding the patient as a whole person may do research on psychological and interpersonal processes as well.

Several new developments were often mentioned by hospital respondents who were excited about their promise for the future. Cost containment is of course important in light of federal government policy at present, but many also saw it as a way to provide good care at less cost to consumers. Recognizing the changing composition of the population, several hospitals are placing special emphasis on care of the elderly. Hospices, providing sensitive attention and support for terminally ill and their families, are a growing part of care for the elderly, though obviously not all their patients are old. Another related development is some form of staged care, in which the intensity of nursing care (etc.) and the amount of self-care varies depending on the needs of the patient and the stage of recovery. Many health care centers are beginning to reach back before treatment with direct preventive medicine programs, including diagnostic screening, health education, and "wellness" education (which usually involves cooperating with schools, businesses, churches, etc. to teach people what they can do to help keep themselves and their families healthy). The teaching and research hospitals emphasize development of new techniques and medical technology, while the rural hospitals emphasize sharing of equipment or cooperative planning with nearby hospitals.

Colleges

The college survey concentrated on the most prevalent form of United Methodist higher education institution, the liberal arts college (though a few of the institutions sampled had another school besides the liberal arts college and two were basically junior colleges). For all of them, the sense of mission is in the provision of solid liberal arts- and values-oriented education. Preparation for leadership is a common way of talking about this process. The secondary emphasis is on community service, primarily through the contributions of graduates to their communities, although some schools have extensive programs of cooperation in community affairs and all see themselves providing services to their immediate communities. (In several instances, the college has the largest payroll in town.)

Interview respondents believe their colleges have much stronger value emphases than schools that are not church-related. They also believe they are less rigid in doctrinal and moral standards and put more emphasis on truth-seeking than colleges related to "conservative" denominations. Most see the core of their work as the liberal arts (with a bias toward preprofessional education), using the relatively small size of the school to provide personalized attention from faculty, administration, and other students. While there is a general trend toward more career-oriented curricula (business administration is the leader in the trend), not all are following it, and those moving in that direction are seeking to keep the breadth and value-orientation of the liberal arts foundation in the career-development emphasis.

These themes are not at all distinctive to United Methodist colleges, but arise frequently when church-related college people talk about what they see as special about their institutions. Indeed, cast as humanistic rather than Christian, the emphasis on values is a rationale often used by private colleges that are not church-related. Another theme common to private schools that is sounded by college respondents in our survey is the importance of the role of private schools as higher education comes to be dominated by state-supported schools. The two aspects of this role most frequently mentioned are (1) providing an alternative to state schools (usually tied to the liberal arts/values emphasis) and (2) putting "leaven into the lump" of higher education by the example of programs and emphases developed in the greater freedom of an independent institution.

Our survey essentially confirms Merriman Cuninggim's judgment on the style of United Methodist colleges. He found essentially three forms of authentic church-relatedness among colleges. (1) The "Covenant College" is an "ally of the church." It shares the basic values of its denomination and finds ways to manifest them and to influence its students with them. However, it does not make a display of its connection, a stance which is also congruent with the denomination's style. (2) The "Proclaiming College" is a "witness for the church." It acknowledges publicly its ties to a denomination and finds ways to manifest those ties, as well as the values involved, to its students. Cuninggim adds, "Once upon a time it witnessed to its own people, faculty and students . . . or . . . to the world outside. . . . Now it may seldom if ever be either the priest or the missionary; it knows itself first as a college, not a religious institution." (3) The "Embodying College" is a "reflection of the church." It tries to reflect soundly the beliefs and practices of its denomination. For it, ecclesiastical faithfulness is the central reality around which higher education revolves.

Cuninggim places most United Methodist colleges in the category of the proclaiming college, with some spillover into the covenant college category. He also notes that there is a spectrum of stances on witness, from those close to that of the embodying college to those close to the ally position. Colleges with independent, "prestige" reputations for liberal arts, colleges that identify very heavily with their community, and research universities seem more likely to be an ally rather than a witness. (Source: Merriman Cuninggim, "Varieties of Church-Relatedness in Higher Education," see *Church-Related Higher Education,* ed., Robert R. Parsonage [Valley Forge: Judson Press, 1978], pp. 17ff., 35.)

Retirement Residences

The sample of retirement homes surveyed portray a basic commitment to provide safe living for elderly persons, though there are many variations on the theme. There is varying emphasis on nursing care: absent in a few, the major function in others. These are varying sizes of homes, from a few residents to hundreds; and the larger homes tend to be more sophisticated in their operations. Finally there is a varying amount of additional programming. Some homes provide residential service and nothing else. Others provide one or more additional services, of which the most common are professional education or training (often in conjunction with a neighboring university), outreach services in churches or persons' homes, and advocacy for older persons' needs (usually done as part of a coalition).

Most of the residences serve the general population of the community or area in which they are located, drawing residents of several religious affiliations. Their residents tend to be seventy-five or older and tend to be from lower or middle income brackets. Many of the homes that began operation earliest had retirement needs of United Methodists as their primary focus, especially "worn-out preachers" and other servants of the church. Indeed, a few homes for retired missionaries and deaconesses still exist. In most homes today, however, the primary service is directed to retired persons in the surrounding community, which may be as large as a section of a state. As outreach services have been growing in importance, homes have more frequently been working as partners with local churches and community agencies in the provision of services.

In summary, what retirement homes do for United Methodism is to provide senior citizens, some of whom may be United Methodists, with options for retirement living. They offer a residence that provides safe, sanitary, and secure housing adapted to the physical and social needs of older people. They offer encouragement for interaction among persons, residents, staff, and volunteers. They see that nourishing food is provided. And increasingly they provide a range of nursing care for those who cannot fully care for themselves but do not need the intensive services of a hospital. From this base of experience, many centers are now reaching out into the community to provide additional group services and to bring services to older persons who want to remain in their own homes and can do so with a little extra help.

Children- and Youth-Serving Agencies

The mission thrust of these agencies is to persons in need, with the primary focus on the children and/or youth themselves and the secondary focus on their parents, but with the final beneficiary being the community. Of the nine agencies surveyed, five reported working with both children and youth, two with youth only, and two with children only (one of the latter two was the only one in the sample to have programming for preschool-age children). Three program only at their own site, while six are involved with outreach programming as well. All but one of the agencies specified that it tried to work with the families of the children and youth.

Typically, the young people for whom they are providing residential care require intensive treatment. In this case, the most frequent source of referral for the young people is the appropriate state agency (e.g. Department of Human Resources). Those departments usually provide funds to pay for the care of the children or youth they send, but in the South there are several agencies that receive very significant support from Annual Conferences and their churches. Some agencies have been moving to help churches and other community groups to develop programs to affect the source of the problems the agencies treat. They are also beginning to work on social change efforts that can help reduce the social base of problems.

While some of these homes include a religious education program as a regular part of their work, the rationale for it is principally as a part of their treatment purpose—to help boys and girls to become mature and productive citizens. Similarly, their involvement in social change is based not on an abstract belief in a better society, but on concern for children and youth and on their specific experience with the young people referred to them. This involvement roughly parallels the growing concern of hospitals with health education and preventive medicine, and it parallels even more closely the role of public health measures in preventing sickness.

Community Centers

As one layman put it, community agencies are "doing something the churches could not do themselves and that otherwise would not be done." That something is an outreach of service into needy communities; that is, helping persons and families to cope with their needs and to overcome the difficulties in their situation. The initial form of that outreach has continued into the present and in most agencies surveyed is being projected into the future. Typical programs are remedial education, training for job skills, preschool education or day care for children of working mothers, building of social skills (through groups, clubs, meetings, etc.), recreation and emergency aid (e.g., distribution of food, clothing, and sometimes money, or provision of emergency shelter for a short time). The specific programs have changed as needs, opportunities, and methods have changed, but the function has held steady.

In recent years these programs of social service have been supplemented with social action efforts which aim to help people to cope better by reducing some of the societal barriers to their opportunity and development. To some degree this trend has continued the tradition of earlier United Methodist activists who struggled to eliminate the liquor traffic that was blighting the lives of many urban poor. These modern community center efforts that advocate political or other social change on behalf of poor people are usually undertaken in coalition with other social work agencies and/or religious groups, including but not limited to United Methodists. A more common form of community center social action has been in community organizing. This activity seeks to help people in disadvantaged communities to get themselves together and identify the power they can bring to bear on their problems. The aim is to help the weak to stand more powerfully to seek better treatment from business and government organizations, as well as political decisions more favorable to their community. Housing, community service, education, and economic development have been frequent concerns.

Miscellaneous Mission

Three other types of agency were included in this study to give some flavor of the rest of the broad range of institutions related to United Methodist conferences and national agencies. (1) Two were multipurpose agencies with a broad range of programs to meet many needs in their communities. (2) Four were special-purpose agencies focusing on a single cluster of needs; two operated through direct provision of services and two used organizing and training to equip others to serve. (3) The other two were residences for persons needing help in social adjustment, a recent and radical change in the nature of their residence use. Some own their own property while others rent.

One key trend in service that became manifest in the interviews about these institutions parallels that found for several other types: movement toward more outreach rather than services only at the primary site of the agency. This trend probably reflects for a given institution the general trend in American society toward deinstitutionalization. Of course, it is also particularly congenial to a church-related approach to initiate contact by reaching out.

Services for United Methodists

While the primary purpose of these institutions, from the perspective of United Methodism, is to minister to needs in the world rather than to help meet needs in the church, many of them do provide special services for United Methodists. For the most part, these special services are not given through the inclusion of United Methodists in the "population" of persons using the basic services of the institutions. In our study, retirement residences and colleges were the only types with significant usage by United Methodists. In 1979 enrollment,

United Methodist colleges and universities ranged from a low of 4 percent to a high of 50 percent of the student body being United Methodist; the average was 24 percent. The low figure, 4 percent, is less than the approximately 6 percent proportion that United Methodists comprise of the total population of the United States. For the homes in our sample, the lowest proportion of United Methodists among residents was 37 percent; the highest was 100 percent; and the median was 75 percent.

Clearly, there is some tendency for United Methodists to want to attend Methodist-related colleges and a much stronger tendency for them to want to use a retirement home related to their denomination. Even in these cases, those choices do not provide a compelling reason by themselves for the institutions to do their ministry. They just demonstrate that United Methodists see the institutions as doing a good job of ministering to the needs of persons, so they take advantage of the services (rarely with reduced rates, unless qualifying under other terms than denomination or under a church-supplied subsidy program).

In addition to inclusion of United Methodist persons in their services, the non-parish institutions all include at least one activity which is provided directly for a United Methodist constituency—though not necessarily exclusively for United Methodists. These activities fall into three basic categories: (1) provision of a tangible point of contact with mission, (2) cooperation in mission activities, and (3) special services for United Methodist groups. A few illustrations of programs involved will best define these categories.

Contact with Mission

Many new hospitals, retirement residences, children's and youth homes, community centers, and many other kinds of non-parish institutions regularly include some forms of voluntary service. While the hospitals and homes tend to organize volunteers through their own volunteer service program or auxiliary, United Methodist churches and especially United Methodist women's groups are primary recruiting grounds. Community centers tend to recruit volunteers through contact with local churches. For each volunteer there is an opportunity to participate in the mission to others' needs, and through the volunteer, there is a chance for the church to which they belong to gain further insight into and feeling for the mission involved. This latter potential is often overlooked in the concentration on the volunteer process as one in which the church helps the institution. The opportunity for learning to move in the other direction must be identified, and ways must be provided to encourage the church to use services offered by the institution.

Another potential service that is often similarly obscured is education on issues relevant to the institution and of concern to United Methodists. Frequently the information shared by institution representatives comes in the context of a presentation seeking support for the institution, i.e., contributions of time and/or money. When that is the case, all involved tend to focus so strongly on the "sales" portion of the message that the independent value of the information is overlooked. Nevertheless, important information is being provided; and in fact, it is often presented through specific workshops under institutional sponsorship or as part of a program for a district, Annual Conference, etc.

When interviewed, many institution administrators and board members, some institution staff, and even a substantial sprinkling of conference persons, pointed to a more general value of mission contact. The sheer presence of an institution doing mission and claiming relationship to United Methodism gave to them a deeper awareness of the church and its people. Some part of this leavening may occur through the reporting and fund-requesting relationships of agencies to Annual Conferences and/or their boards, but for the most part it seems to be left to a hoped-for osmosis, a permeation from institution to church without any particular effort on the part of either. For instance, one college president spoke of Methodist colleges as an "intellectual headlight for the Church." However, there are very few communication channels to connect the beam of that headlight with the church's present and future needs, or to identify critical discoveries and specifically call them to the attention of decision-makers in United Methodism. The value of the college's work to the church depends on a series of informal personal communication channels leading by good luck or God's grace to the helpful information being in the right place at the right time.

Cooperation in Mission Activities

Our survey reveals two major types of program involving this function. Other than colleges and hospitals, all types of institutions work with other United Methodist groups (often as a part of a broader ecumenical or community effort) to influence community and government decisions. The institutions provided government contacts, through their involvement with a variety of state and other governmental bodies and through information derived from their own work. Frequently, community centers also provide contact with similarly concerned groups in the community with other institutions serving to link the appropriate professional or interagency organization for "lobbying" efforts. Sometimes agency representatives participate directly in this lobbying, and sometimes they provide the information and contacts for other activist units of the church to use. In either event, the institutions provide resources for United Methodist social action projects.

An apparently increasing aspect of cooperation takes the form of consultation by agency personnel with local churches or other United Methodist bodies to help them to develop their program. For colleges and hospitals, this process tends to be an informal one using college faculty or hospital professional personnel with appropriate expertise either as paid or volunteer consultants. The same informal process happens in other agencies, but in them, some formal assignment of staff time by the agency to work with a specific potential United

Methodist program occurs. For instance, a local church trying to develop a program of home visitation by active senior citizens to homebound elders could get advice from the staff of a nearby retirement residence.

Special Services

Colleges (and to a much lesser degree, other types of institutions) frequently provide space for United Methodist activities. Annual Conferences meet on campuses, United Methodist historical libraries and other archives are often housed on campuses, and frequently land or building space is made available for location of conference offices. Colleges, especially, also put together continuing education programs for clergy and laity, but all types of institutions frequently offer such programming for churches in their vicinity. Chaplaincy programs, particularly if the chaplain is United Methodist by policy, are another service colleges and hospitals offer. It is the relationship of the chaplaincy program to United Methodist clergy that constitutes the special service in this case. Finally, some colleges and hospitals provide special services to United Methodist clergy and their families, with special scholarships for college and special discounts on hospital charges being the most common.

This chapter has attempted to describe the nature of the mission being performed, not preempt the judgment of whether any specific aspect of mission is needed or any specific institution is needed for it to be satisfactorily performed, nor yet to discuss whether relationship between United Methodism and that institution is really important. We will turn to those questions soon, but first we need to look at the factors of change that shape the nature of current United Methodist concern.

CHAPTER 4

Why Should We Be Concerned Now?

United Methodist-related institutions have developed through the patterns and for the purposes outlined in the last two chapters. Now, however, many persons in the church and in the institutions are asking questions about the relationship—and rightly so. Major trends of change are provoking those questions, and those trends mean that the time has come for serious rethinking of the role the institutions play for United Methodism and the forms their relationship should take. Those trends are affecting the life of the church and the place of the institutions in society. Thus the answer to the question of why we should now be concerned follows from the answer to two other questions: (1) What is happening to the church? (2) What is happening to the institutions?

What Is Happening to the Church?

Many trends are of course developing in the church, most of which affect its relationship with institutions only tangentially; however, three trends bear directly on that issue. First, the church is experiencing growing constraints on its ability to help the institutions, at least financially. Second, United Methodists have in the past and will in the future be constantly discovering new needs to be met. Third, there is a central philosophical revolution occurring in the church's approach to its outreach through services.

Financial constraints are reflected in feelings among United Methodists that the survival of many of their churches is threatened and by the growing complexity of the role and survival of non-parish institutions. The survival threat has two components, loss and morale. While giving by United Methodists has been rising steadily, churches have been hard pressed to keep pace with inflation. Thus, most churches are feeling themselves less able to cover rising costs with contributions, let alone undertake extra fund-raising for denominational or institutional purposes. At the same time, many churches have been experiencing erosion in their membership.

In other words, many churches are feeling a loss in their power to survive and be in significant ministry. That sense of loss of power contributes inevitably to the weakening of morale among leadership and members. There is widespread doubt among United Methodist leaders that the church will be able to find ways to surmount the challenges of change that confront it and produce reinvigorated life and ministry. (See two earlier studies in this series: Alan K. Waltz, *Images of the Future* and William E. Ramsden, *The Church in a Changing Society,* both published in 1980 by Abingdon.)

Another assault on morale comes as church leaders try to relate to non-parish institutions. They find the specific situation in which the institution works is too complex for them to be able to understand it readily or to deal effectively with the problems involved. Each institution has a range of issues it confronts which require special technical competence— knowledge and skills. Most United Methodists quickly become aware of their lack of that competence when they try to deal with those issues. Partly as a result of the institutions' needs for special skills and partly as a consequence of churches' interests being focused much more on their own survival issues or their own commitments to mission, there is not very much direct contact between churches and institutions. This lack of direct contact makes it too easy to miss the fact that under the technical issues there are questions of values and mission that can be a mutual base for meaningful dialogue on "real questions" between institutions and churches.

New needs in the community to which the church could respond are constantly being discovered by persons concerned for outreach. Almost always these discoveries pick up areas of need that are not being met—or at least not met well—by other resources in the community. Sometimes these needs relate to an expanding or changing program of an existing institution. Sometimes they can be met by direct action by local churches. Or sometimes they lead to the need for a new non-parish institution. Either of the latter two developments will produce new competition for the attention and support that the older institutions have been receiving.

A *changing philosophy of service* has particularly affected two dimensions of United Methodist concern and ideas related to non-parish institutions. The earlier approach of direct services to persons seems to be waning before an approach that aims to improve persons' abilities to get their needs met, which sets helping them to help themselves above provision of services.

On the world scene, this trend has meant a shift from sending missionaries to do outreach for The United Methodist Church to providing assistance (including missionary person-nel) to third-world churches to help them minister in their own countries. On the domestic social service and action scene, this trend has meant a relative growth in importance of empowerment as compared to direct services.

At the same time, there has been growing acceptance of the priority of the public sector in meeting social service needs. The basic commitment of the church in creating non-parish institutions was to meet community needs. The trend of empowerment and the ethics of justice both suggest that the needs of a community should be met through the collective efforts of the whole community. Thus, tax-supported efforts are seen as an appropriate expression of Christian concern. Consequently, United Methodists do not feel that concerns for meeting needs are preempted if a public agency takes the place of a United Methodist agency in that task.

Obviously, these observations are trends and are stated in terms of the directions in which those trends are evolving. Not all United Methodists would agree with any of the positions just outlined, but there does seem to be substantial movement in the directions indicated. Each of these trends has the effect of reducing involvement by church members with existing non-parish institutions.

What Is Happening to the Institutions?

Meanwhile, the institutions have been affected just as deeply by a number of changes in their social environment. One set of changes relates to the development of networks of private and public agencies having the same general purposes and to the appearance of a variety of regulatory agencies in local, state, and federal governments. Often United Methodist agencies have been in the forefront of movements seeking better standards for organizations involved in their field, since leaders of those agencies have been concerned for the welfare not only of their own participants (patients, students, residents, clients, etc.), but also for other persons in similar need. In any event, most non-parish institutions are now accountable to at least one and often more than a dozen governmental and professional organizations for meeting a wide range of standards and regulations. These other accountabilities draw the agency's attention away from its connection to United Methodism, at least to some degree. In our survey we found very few institution personnel who thought their organization would change its philosophy of service if its relationship to United Methodism were to be severed. However, many would have to stop operating altogether if they were not in compliance with the demands of regulatory bodies.

In addition, broad social changes have been sweeping through American society in recent years that have had great impact on non-parish institutions. For instance, every institution has felt the dual impact of inflation and rising expectations of level and quality of service. Improved services usually involve increased costs, and those increases are multiplied by overall inflation resulting in a major cost-containment problem for most agencies. Five other general trends have had an impact on non-parish institutions.

1. Since World War II, one of the major demographic changes was the baby boom of the 1950s followed by a steady decline in the birth rate thereafter. As a consequence of that shift, the number of babies born has decreased annually for about twenty years. That downtrend's first wave of children is just now attaining college age. Meanwhile the children of the baby boom are now young adults, and their changing concerns bring changing emphases to social needs, to markets for business goods and services, and even to advertising.

2. Largely due to improved health measures, the number of retired persons has been increasing steadily, and will probably continue to increase (though at a slightly lower rate) even as the smaller crop of depression babies hits retirement age later this century. Two consequences are involved. On the one hand, people are active and able to be self-supporting for more years. On the other hand, more persons live longer years, necessitating higher levels of care from others for a fairly lengthy span of time (but not usually commencing until age seventy-five or so).

3. Wives and mothers who are gainfully employed are becoming the norm rather than the exception. One consequence is a steadily rising need for day care services for the young children of working mothers. Another is a shift in national expectations from providing sustenance to fatherless families through welfare to enabling mothers to work. Also, a return to work by a married woman often means a preliminary return to education to take advantage of expanding career opportunities for women.

4. For at least a decade one of the major trends in social service has been deinstitutionalization (so-called by the professionals who run institutions or by the government bodies that try to influence them). It reflects the discovery that many people who were in institutions could do as well or better if they were not kept in institutions. It may also reflect the general national attitude of decreased confidence and trust in institutions. In the religious arena, the growth of "the electronic church" as an alternative to membership in a congregation probably reflects this underlying social trend.

5. A central trend in health-care parallels the deinstitutionalization trend. Major health-care professions and institutions are being put into context and seen as means of caring for the sick. Responsibility for health promotion and preservation is seen as the responsibility of individual, family, and community. Sound public health measures and improved life-style habits have become vital frontiers in the contemporary struggle to improve health.

Consider the impact on institutions of the five trends just mentioned.

Hospitals are moving to build much more effective programs of service for older people, and aging is becoming a major focus of their research. Also, they are beginning to offer their justification to society in terms of their backup role ("tertiary care"), and they seek to add as much as they can of the latest equipment and technologies to put quality into that function. On the other hand, there is growing involvement with and support for health education and decentralized treatment centers.

Colleges are facing significant enrollment drops in the 1980s, at least from traditional college-age students. The general population movement to the sunbelt makes this drop potentially much more severe for schools in the Northeast and North Central areas, while schools in the sunbelt will probably receive sufficient population in-migration to compensate for the national decrease in the number of student-age persons (particularly true for the West Coast and Mountain states, and for Texas and Florida). On the other hand, opportunities for students older than the traditional age, particularly on a part-time basis could be greatly expanded. Mothers (and other women) seeking education to become qualified for a better job and active retired persons seeking intellectual stimulation offer two new large sources of students. Those schools involved with the training of persons for the health-care professions will need to provide information, support, and values for their students to deal with the changing scene in health care. Also, special attention to the knowledge and value base for lifelong self-care to promote health would seem to be a particularly appropriate aspect of a liberal arts education.

Retirement residences face two contradictory realities. On the one hand, there is and will be a growing need for their services. Those seeking admission will tend to be older (at least seventy-five) and may well be needing increased medical attention not too long after admission. On the other hand, the younger and more vigorous retired persons will want to continue to live on their own. For many of those persons there is a period of transition when special services of support to supplement self-care will be needed in their own homes. Thus, retirement homes need to be preparing for expanded admissions and a much heavier call on nursing services, and at the same time, they need to reach out into the community and into people's homes to supply supplementary services.

Children- and youth-serving agencies have been shielded from a potential enrollment drop due to the lower birth rate only by their shift in focus to more severely troubled young people. Their role in this regard is roughly parallel to that of hospitals, the last stop on the road to seeking help. With the increase in working mothers (and in single-parent families), the needs and opportunities for outreach in offices, neighborhoods, family education, and community development efforts are growing rapidly.

Community centers face increased demands for child-care and early childhood education with the increased number of young adults and the increasing proportion of working mothers among them. As job-holding expectations spread, career and job-getting skills become important training concerns. Needs to empower adults and to help community economic development are on the rise. In addition, many community centers face needs to assist street people who would have been in various institutions a decade or more ago but who are now on their own—and still needing special attention and support from time to time.

In all these ways—and probably many more once the impact of economic change and population movement are taken into account both for direct and indirect effects—United Methodism's non-parish institutions are being buffeted by strong contemporary trends. Furthermore, they are particularly sensitive to such changes because their basic style is to respond to needs and to adapt as needs change.

With the church feeling more constrained in helping yet at the same time facing constantly unfolding needs and shifts in philosophy, and with institutions confronted with the need for continuing adaptation as their situations change, many feel uneasy with the present arrangements between United Methodism and its institutions. The time has come to review relationships, missions, and commitments.

CHAPTER 5

Do We Really Need
All Those Institutions?

There are really two issues tied together in this question. One is whether the institutions are still needed to meet the needs which have been their mission, including the issue of whether those needs are still worth meeting. The other is whether, in those cases in which institutions are needed, the institutions or the church needs to have the relationship of the institution to United Methodism continued, and what form it should take if it is to be continued. Each of those questions deserves a chapter of its own, so this chapter will address whether institutions are needed, while the question of relationship will be considered in the following chapter.

When the question of whether institutions are needed is left in the abstract, the answer is simple. Yes, complex needs require the special attention that only institutions can give and sustain. But when it is asked if all such institutions are needed, the answer is equally clearly no. In any group as large as that of United Methodist-related institutions, it is certain that some could be discontinued without seriously undercutting the likelihood that persons with the needs to which it ministers could still get help. In fact, it is probable that the coming decade will see some institutions disband, others merge, and still others make radical changes in function (in effect becoming new agents of mission while maintaining institutional continuity).

The question really becomes meaningful when it is put specifically: Is this particular institution still needed, given the present situation? Ordinarily this question would only be asked at a time of crisis, when the future viability of the institution is in question. Except under those circumstances, United Methodism supplies too small a proportion of most agencies' budgets to be able to raise life and death questions.

Even in the case of institutions whose boards are named officially by Annual Conferences or whose property is owned by a United Methodist body, an agency determined to stay in operation with support from other segments of the community would usually be able to continue. In other words, most of the time the question to which United Methodists and their institutions can seek answers is the question of relationship rather than the question of institutional survival.

Nevertheless, the next few years will surely bring some United Methodist-related institutions into life-and-death emergencies. At such times, the operating question for the church is, "Shall we try to rescue this specific institution?" The rescue could be attempted by provision of special financial aid, or it could be sought through bringing to bear the denomination's "good offices"; that is, United Methodism could use its connections with other private sources such as local churches, foundations, or similar agencies and its contacts in local, state, and national government bodies to convince them to do certain specific things which would give the United Methodist institution new resources. Of course, both types of assistance could be offered.

Should this question be faced, there are a few general principles suggested by this study which could help to focus that deliberation.

1) An institution that is in trouble because of lack of response to its services is probably not needed. Either its diagnosis of needs or its methods of meeting them are not adequate for the persons it seeks to serve, or perhaps it has failed to find a way to communicate to those persons what it really has to offer. Especially if other somewhat similar institutions in the community are viable, the one in danger of failing is probably not needed. One alternative explanation is that the institution in question is suffering from mismanagement, and the board

and administration should be changed. If there is any possibility of alternative help available for the institution's users, the burden of proof should rest strongly on those who would want to "bail out" a mismanaged institution.

2) If United Methodists become involved in considering a rescue, the likelihood is that a number of secular bodies are also involved in the situation. Coordination of data-gathering and assessment of the situation with them will be advisable, and may be a necessity. Each United Methodist-related institution is also related to a variety of secular agencies that supply funds and/or regulate compliance of practices with the law or with professional ethical standards. The range and strength of those relationships for all types of institutions in our survey was greater than relations with United Methodists.

3) An institution may be in trouble because government funding has been withdrawn. Such a crisis usually focuses on continuing a specific program rather than the viability of the whole agency, but loss of funding for a central program could threaten its survivability. Here again, the decision to rescue depends upon the value found in the program for the persons served by it.

Each of these judgments is based on the general feeling of this survey that institution management is very sensitive to the need to cope with changing circumstances in order to survive and be effective. Thus, when the institution comes into a time of emergency, either of two circumstances exists. (1) There has already been a serious breakdown in its own systems of identifying change and adapting to it. If the need were evident to others and the institution were doing its job of effective administration and fund-finding for needed programs, the chances of a life-threatening emergency would not be very great. (2) There has been a major change in the institution's environment which makes its services irrelevant or greatly reduces the need for them. For those reasons, the focus of United Methodist decision-making should be on the groups served by the agency, and the institution should be held responsible to show documented evidence of its value and necessity.

For instance, the more a college needs financial support from the church, the less likely it is to deserve that support. Good management and good recruitment will meet prudent budgets. It would only be service to special persons who would not otherwise have access to higher education that could be an overriding factor. Even then, United Methodists should analyze whether it would in the long run be less costly to provide direct supplementary subsidies for the potential students rather than pouring money into a college. Of course, the colleges all need contributions and should be expected to seek them from United Methodists (and others).

Similarly, a retirement residence in trouble for lack of residents is clearly not needed, but programs of support for self-care or community-based ministries to the elderly might warrant ongoing support. Or, if a community center were to lose funds for its involvement in controversial action on behalf of its clients or community, it would probably deserve some temporary special aid to give it a chance to rebuild its credibility with its other supporters or to find new sources of funding.

Since the purpose served for United Methodism by its related institutions is reaching out to persons' needs, phasing out an agency would be a time when special efforts by the church would be necessary, focused on helping persons to find alternative ways to meet the needs with which the agency had been helping. That would be true whether the involvement had been with individuals, families, or larger groups. The United Methodist Church would want the persons involved to know that the phase out of an agency was not the result of indifference to them on the part of the church.

While, as noted above, an institution might be able to find ways to continue even if the church wanted it to cease operating, there could be value in periodic reviews of the real need for the agency and its services. Certainly that can be required of those owned and/or operated directly by a United

Methodist body. Something more than an annual budget-review process would be needed. Clear evaluation standards and expected levels of performance would need to be established well in advance. Setting such a process on a regular schedule (e.g., every five years) would permit evaluation and decision-making in something other than a crisis atmosphere. It would probably result in decisions for changes much less drastic than a phase-out, if the process were done in an open and objective manner. The data developed would provide clear direction for agency planning and encourage a style of more rapid adjustment to changing situations. Furthermore, the regular review with those institutions would help to reduce the inertia of relationship to other agencies (the "We've *always* had them, of course we shall continue with them" assumption). In other words, evaluating even a few agencies could well lead to other evaluations of the advisability of sustaining a relationship where there is no accountability for United Methodism to question the institution's continuation.

CHAPTER 6

Should We Still Be Related? If So, How?

By its very nature, a relationship exists because it is desired or at least tolerated by the parties to it. That is true for starting a relationship, and, as the rising divorce rate demonstrates, must be true for sustaining a relationship. "United Methodist-related" carries the implication that the institution so designated and at least one United Methodist body want that relationship to exist. The departure of such colleges and universities as Western Maryland, Northwestern, and Vanderbilt from relationship with United Methodism shows that for many institutions severance of relationship can be achieved essentially unilaterally. The church's role in those partings was principally one of accepting the school's intention. Presumably, the appropriate unit of the church could also unilaterally take action to sever a relationship, if an institution were to take a similar passive role of acceptance. However, it seems more likely that church bodies would discuss the situation together with their institution and arrive at a mutually acceptable decision to sever the relationship (or to maintain it).

That discussion and decision would need to be specific for each relationship between a United Methodist body and an institution. This survey did not gather sufficient data to make suggestions on the future for any one of the agencies that participated in it. However, certain general points have become manifest which can help give direction to any particular consideration of whether to continue or to terminate a relationship between a United Methodist body and an institution.

Since such relationships normally tend to perpetuate themselves (at least formally) if left untouched, the burden of proof, practically speaking, would usually be on severance. In some cases, this tendency would be reinforcd by legal consideration; for instance, the agency may be owned by The United Methodist Church, or the relationship may be written into the institution's corporate charter and bylaws. In other cases, there may be no legal constraint, but a strong feeling of moral responsibility to stay together once having come into relationship. Quite possibly there is a parental quality to this feeling on the part of the church—it helped to create the institution and would not feel right about deserting its offspring. There could also be a wide range of psychological and political assumptions and considerations that would tend to keep the relationship intact, at least in name. Thus, once the issue of severance is raised, the question would be "Why should we sever or change our relationship?"

Nevertheless, the issue deserves careful consideration. The basic answer to "Why sever?" is simply that one or both parties has concluded that it is the best thing to do. A United Methodist body might want the financial or administrative freedom that severance would bring—freedom to shift funding or staff and volunteer effort to other institutions and/or programs. Or, it might conclude that it would be a more honest statement of the true situation between church and institution to have no claim to relationship. Conversely, an institution might want greater freedom to relate to a number of religious groups equally, or it might feel that it could do better in other relationships more important to it without the United Methodist relationship (e.g, with governmental or private secular funding agencies).

In fact, the question that will provide the best data on whether to sever is: "Why stay in relationship?" A decision on continuing or severing must be made in light of the reasons, if any, that the church and the institution have for being in relationship. If those benefits are not worth their cost to one or both parties, then the relationship has become a liability. A few key reasons for relationship appear to be typical from our survey.

Typical Reasons for Relating

One layman commented, "Historically The United Methodist Church has founded institutions at points of need. Then, when the institutions get their feet on the ground, it withdraws." He might have added that it withdraws to give them room to operate, but it does not disclaim them. The relationship is sustained because the denominational parent is proud of its child (now grown up) or because it feels the need to be ready to help. The institution, correspondingly, may look upon the tie as an affirmation of the founding spirit behind it, as a part of the tradition of the place. This tradition of operation is usually embodied in three ways: (1) the legal relationship of institution and church, (2) the composition of the board of the agency, and (3) the concern of the board to be responsive to United Methodist goals. As table 1 shows, each of these factors is manifest in a variety of relationships, although the degree of closeness varies from one type of institution to another when measured on this scale.

Our survey found that in many cases financial assistance from church sources to institutions was important for United Methodism as well as for institutions. Agency personnel often commented on the importance to them of token budgetary support and sometimes identified specific aspects of program made possible by an Annual Conference contribution or (more likely) by contributions secured from local churches with the blessing of a conference. One hospital board chairperson said, "We told the Conference that we did not need any money designated for us in their budget; it's just a token to us and could be of real help to some other agency. But they told us that if we weren't in the budget they would soon forget about us. So we're still in the budget." Thus, the giving and receiving of mission support is another reason relationships are continued.

TABLE 1. Closeness of Relationship Between Institution and Denomination in Terms of Board Selection and Composition, and Goal Determination. Percentage of respondents from each institutional type, identifying each level of relationship.

	Total	Hospital	College	Retirement	Child/Youth	Community	Misc.
Branch or unit of UMC body—"owned and operated."	27.4	11.1	14.5	20.9	48.7	40.0	50.0
Selected by UMC body; clear accountability to UMC body.	19.6	33.3	16.9	39.5	23.1	2.2	0
Selected by UMC body; no clear accountability to UMC body.	7.0	22.2	6.0	7.0	5.1	2.2	0
Independently named with UMC majority; special concern for UMC goals.	17.8	13.9	18.1	18.6	18.0	17.8	20.8
Independently named with UMC minority; special concern for UMC goals.	10.4	0	15.7	0	0	22.2	20.8
Independently named with UMC majority; no special concern for UMC goals.	6.7	13.9	8.4	11.6	2.6	0	0
Independently named with UMC minority; no special concern for UMC goals.	8.5	2.8	14.5	2.3	2.6	15.6	4.2
No special UMC inclusion; some special concern for UMC goals.	1.1	0	2.4	0	0	0	4.2
No special UMC inclusion; no special concern for UMC goals.	1.5	2.8	3.6	0	0	0	0

In fact, our survey found a more potent level of the interest-investment dynamic. The institutions that seemed to have the closest relationships to United Methodists in the local churches of a conference were those that raised a significant part of their budget by some type of "advance special" giving. They had conference permission to approach congregations directly for contributions, and the churches received recognition from the conference for the resulting gifts. This arrangement brought frequent contact, relatively high levels of information flow from agency to churches, more awareness on the part of church members of the agency and its work, and more pride in that work.

On the other hand, budget support ranked lowest of the factors we asked respondents to rate for their importance to the institution in relating to United Methodism. As chart 1 shows, tradition was by far most frequently seen as important. Public identity of the institution as United Methodist was next, but significantly lower than the rating given tradition. Charters requiring linkage were next most important, but it must be remembered that the charters reflect the beginnings of an institution and may not portray very accurately its present commitments. Commitment to purposes involved in their certification is a current reflection, and these are fairly heavily seen as embodiments of United Methodist goals. Of similar importance to the institution is access through the denomination to individual donors. Much less important is access to participants. (This factor was higher by colleges, however.) Budget, at the bottom, shows very little importance at all. Other results showed relatively little influence by Annual Conferences on institution policy or hiring and promotion decisions and only occasional helpfulness in dealings with regulators, lenders, foundations, etc.

Interviews with persons in the conferences who were not affiliated with the institutions clearly identified the basic mission or service of the agency as the reason for United Methodists to be related. Their response must, of course, be seen in context. Respondents showed no sign of urging

Chart 1. Importance of Factors Causing Institutions to Sustain Their Relationships with The United Methodist Church

K
E ☐ Percentage rating as relatively important
Y
   ■ Percentage rating as relatively unimportant

FACTORS

The institution's certification focuses on purposes which are specifically identified as fulfilling United Methodist mission.

United Methodist sources supply basic budgetary support.

Linkage is required by the institution's charter.

United Methodist channels provide access to potential patients, students, clients, or participants.

United Methodist channels provide access to individual donors.

United Methodist relationship is part of the institution's public identity.

The institution has been traditionally related to The United Methodist Church.

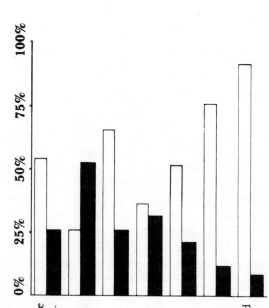

relationship with any additional agencies performing the same mission, so their affirmation of institution goals is set within the tradition of relationship between institution and church. A secondary value mentioned by a few respondents was favorable public relations coming to United Methodism from association with the good job done by an institution.

One set of questions on the survey questionnaire asked people to rate whether they thought the relationships between institutions and The United Methodist Church should be closer or more distant. Three dimensions of relationship were surveyed: financial responsibility, administrative responsibility, and mutual understanding and values. As chart 2 shows, the overall trend of the three sets of responses points to positive feelings about the relationship, but the differences among the three are even more significant. The desire for greater closeness in terms of mutual understanding and values is overwhelming, with at least two-thirds of the respondents for each type of institution indicating they wanted closer affiliation. At the other extreme, child/youth agencies and community centers were the only types of institutions indicating a desire for closer affiliation in terms of administrative control. Finally, in terms of financial responsibility, hospitals were the only institutional type that produced significantly less than half its respondents wanting closer affiliation; but the whole range of scores was lower for this dimension than for mutual understanding and values.

Interview comments suggest that the financial-responsibility dimension was seen differently by institution-related respondents and conference-related respondents. The former seemed to be thinking primarily in terms of the denomination taking more responsibility for its institutions and the latter in terms of the institutions being more responsible to the denomination in the way they used their funds. Therefore, this scale should probably not be given quite as much weight as its numbers suggest.

It is clear that financial responsibility is desired more than administrative control. Both these dimensions, however, pose

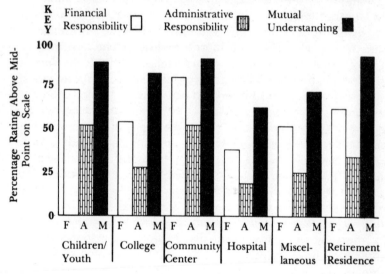

Chart 2. Percentage of Respondents Rating Above the Mid-point for Desire for More Closeness Between Institutions and The United Methodist Church in terms of Financial Responsibility, Administrative Responsibility, Mutual Understanding and Values, and Type of Institution.

the same dilemma for an Annual Conference because there really is no best way to exercise ongoing accountability. At best, only a small measure of accountability is provided through annual reports to conference sessions. Such contacts are not adequate, however, to a close relationship of financial responsibility. Sensing that problem undoubtedly influenced both agency and conference respondents to want to avoid attempting closer relationship. Of course the desire not to meddle (or to be meddled with) entered in as well.

The interviews underline the primacy of mutual understanding and relating more closely on values. When asked if there would be any change in the philosophy and operations of their institution if its relationship to The United Methodist Church were somehow to be terminated, almost every respondent said they thought it would not change, since it was already built into the structure of the agency and the approach of its staff. Those who identified possible changes all expressed concern that the values of humanity and service would erode if it were not for the supportive relationship of the church. It was a hospital administrator (the type of institution usually indicating least closeness) who said: "I'm afraid that in time our capacity to sustain a genuinely humane stance would shrivel, and we'd become sterile—just like the rest of the health-care industry."

This set of reasons for relationships can give a framework within which discussion of any given United Methodist/institution relationship can be focused. The data involved, however, point clearly to the primary focus being on the mission task which the institution performs on behalf of the church. The critical question of relationship is at this point. The church must decide if it wants its name and support attached to an institution devoted to those purposes, and it must determine if the approach taken by the particular agency in working on those goals is consistent with the values the church wants to support.

If the decision on goals and methods is positive, and if the institution sees value in being related to The United Methodist Church, then the question turns to how the relationship can be sustained. It may be that in working on the means of relationship it will become clear to either the church or the institution that the effort required to make the relationship a real one is more than the benefits of relating are worth. In that case, the decision would be not to relate.

Partners in Relationship

The key to effective future relationships between United Methodism and institutions is the concept of partnership. If the institutions were children of the church, they are clearly now adult children. As such they require a relationship appropriate between adults. Family affection and loyalty is still to be expected; but parental rights to punish and instruct, parental obligations to support, children's obligations to be obedient, and children's rights to be dependent are no longer appropriate. It is as if one's child has gone off to college and graduate school and is now back in town as a practicing professional. A close relationship is in the interest of each, but both sides need respect as adults. In this case, the analogy leads to a professional practice that can in some sense complement that of the parents, otherwise no special relationship is needed. When adults want to cooperate around ventures of mutual benefit, the basic form is partnership.

An effective partnership between United Methodism and a related institution will require mutual clarity on the expectations each has of the other. Each will need to agree on what it will give to the other and what it will hold the other responsible to give to it. Then there will be mutual accountability, but accountability within the terms agreed on in creating the partnership and honored because of the value of the partnership.

In general, institutions cannot expect major funding from the church, but United Methodist bodies should be open to considering a partner's request for specific support for a specific program, along with all the other requests for financial help. A new basis of mutual sharing is needed to shift the focus away from funding. This basis should give United Methodism a way to be involved with related institutions, supportive of their mission, and able to learn from their experience. It should also give each institution a clear channel to offer input, make requests, and engage in dialogue.

An institution's primary contribution would be its mission of service; its "business" is its mission, and performance of that mission embodies the United Methodist outreach of caring service to the needs of the world. Thus, a partner institution would be agreeing to identify its service as representative of United Methodist concern (though it would not need to make this an exclusive identification). Secondarily, the institution could provide from its operation data that would help United Methodism to shape the direction of its ministry and mission. The institution could also provide some specific training or consultation to help in the church's development of its program when that development relates to the institution's expertise.

United Methodism's role in the partnership would begin by affirming the institution's basic activity as an expression of Christian mission. That general affirmation could be expressed through such specific efforts as (1) developing programs of dialogue between institution and church people on the value issues the institution is confronting; or (2) using its contacts and credibility to help the institution get access to such sources of contributions as individuals and foundations and to such means of communication to the public as the media.

Conference and national boards can help to create and sustain networks of United Methodist-related institutions with similar functions and problems, much as several national units, particularly the Health and Welfare Division, have done. Those networks can identify effective models that are working in one or more institutions and make them available to the others in the network. They can also provide technical assistance in the form of consultants to help an institution try to solve one or more of the problems it confronts. The outreach program director of one retirement residence might consult with staff (and perhaps a committee of the board) of another residence to help them plan a new program of services to be offered for persons in their own homes. Networks functioning in that way are a prime example of partnership. Communication links among networks of different kinds of institutions and between them and the networks of local churches in conferences and various program agencies would enable points for cooperation to be identified. Then, those who want to cooperate can find one another and start to work. For instance, a congregation interested in ministering more fully to the needs of its older members could hear about and become a part of the program of outreach being planned by the retirement residence. Thus, institution expertise could be made available to assist congregations and others who are seeking to follow through on new challenges for service.

While the information and technical assistance interchange is essential to a partnership, the basic mutual benefit is at a deeper level. At heart, the central value of the relationship is integrity in mission. A partner institution seeks connection with the church to help it face issues of values and keep performance of its mission based in the loving concern of Christian community. A partner-church relates to institutions to help keep in touch with a sense of mission that transcends its own institutional survival worries.

When those benefits of partnership are not able to be realized by either the church or the institution or both, that fact is strong evidence that the relationship is not functional. The two parties would then need to decide whether they wanted to sustain the formality of relationship for old time's sake or to name the reality of the present and recognize lack of function by severing their tie. When some benefits can be achieved, but their potential is largely being left untapped, that is a symptom of a relationship needing priority attention by both church and institution. Each party would then have to consider whether it was worth the effort to them to vitalize the relationship. A decision that is not worth the effort would argue strongly for severance of the relationship in recognition of its low value to the presumed partners.

For instance, mutual understanding and values was the major area in which closer relationships between United Methodism and its institutions was desired. Although this was the case for colleges and for hospitals as well as the other institutional types, these two types consistently rated lowest on all the measures of closeness in our survey. College personnel mentioned values as a distinctive aspect of their mission more frequently than any of the others, and hospital-related respondents pointed to such value issues for them as patients' rights, balancing cost control and quality care priorities, and insuring the right to needed care for all regardless of their personal means to pay. Clearly, there is a basis for special seminars to consider these value issues (or their equivalents in colleges) that would bring people from the institutions and United Methodist clergy and laity into dialogue. If a conference and its related hospital or college is not able to develop and successfully conduct such seminars or an alternative method of dealing collaboratively with the value issues, they should reconsider whether they ought to be claiming a relationship that cannot be expressed in meaningful partnership.

A relationship that has no other clear embodiment than a token contribution from a church budget to an institution can be no more than a token relationship. However, the history of United Methodist/institution relations has been more than token. The church has created agencies, watched over, prayed for, and nurtured them with intense sustenance. As they have grown in strength, developing and exercising their autonomy, institutions have moved away from substantial dependence upon the church. Now, the issue is to choose between three basic options: (1) work to define and express a new and maturely fulfilling partnership, (2) be satisfied with tokenism, or (3) admit the lack of real value in the relationship and sever it.

Even casting the choices that starkly leaves one other issue of relationship unresolved, and it must be considered before much benefit can be gained from a discussion of what the future may hold. The question of relationship between institution and United Methodism involves two parties. It is always clear who the corporate relating party is on the institutional side—it is the institution itself. There may be little clarity on what persons are relating on behalf of the institution, but there is no doubt about the institution itself. On the other hand, that clarity does not always exist on the United Methodist side; there are often several church bodies involved in the relationship. Not only may there be confusion on who the personal representative should be, but there is often uncertainty about which body really speaks for United Methodism.

Our survey showed that most institutions relate to either an Annual Conference or one of its boards or agencies, or to a national board or one of its agencies, or to both conference and national levels. For most agencies, the conference level seemed to take priority. However, health and welfare agencies often had legal ties to Annual Conferences through their boards but related more closely in communication and activity with national agencies, particularly the Division of Health and Welfare Ministries. It would seem that the usual situation is one in which the institution is formally related in some fashion to the Annual Conference, reports to or otherwise relates to at least one Annual Conference board or committee, belongs to at least one network of similar agencies which is a project of a national board, and may relate directly to United Methodist Women, at least on the conference, and perhaps on the national, level.

Because of this situation, the decision to sever or build a relationship would have to be made for each one of those ties. If the institution took the initiative in saying, "We do not want to be United Methodist-related any more," all the ties would probably be severed. On the other hand, if any one United Methodist body were to evaluate its relationship with an institution and seek to enter discussions with it to find ways to vitalize the connection or decide to end it, the resulting decision would not be binding on any of the other relating units of United Methodism. All units would need to participate in the process, agree to make the outcome a consensus decision by which all would abide, and then actually follow it through with action to get full commitment or severance from United Methodism. While that latter course is desirable, even piecemeal action by various agencies would better prepare church and institutions to face the uncertain future.

CHAPTER 7

What Can We Expect Next?

Any attempt to rethink relationships between United Methodism and its related non-parish institutions will need to reckon with the changes the immediate future will bring. Indeed, those changes could even bring reconsideration of some relationships that are now taken for granted. While any basic trend in American society could affect institution/church relationships, we can concentrate on five predictions dealing directly with those relationships. They are highly probable and can confidently be used.

1. There will be continuing change in the social environment which the church and the institutions share. These social changes will involve significant shifts in the needs to which institutions respond and will alter the constraints and the opportunities for United Methodist action to help meet such needs. The directions, timing, and particulars of any of these changes are very difficult to predict, but that they will come in some way at some time in the next few years is certain.

2. As conditions change, institutions will adapt their program, their style, or even their self-definition to meet new configurations of need. Some will be more responsive than others, and those that are slow to respond may find their existence threatened if they fall out of step with current needs. One dimension of institution style is closeness to United Methodism, and some agencies will probably decide they would like to be more closely affiliated to be better able to respond to new needs. Others may for the same reason want greater distance or even severed relationship.

3. With varying needs and opportunities, a variety of potential points for new institutions will appear. Realization of needs or opportunities to minister to them will elicit new programs from local churches, Annual Conferences, and other United Methodist bodies. Some of those program ideas will be managed by the church's organization, some will be referred to one or more of the non-parish institutions, but some will become the kernels of new non-parish institutions.

4. Given such trends as deinstitutionalization and health self-care, many of the needs and opportunities to respond will appear within the fellowship and organizational scope of local churches. Functions that have long been delegated to specialized institutions (e.g. health support) will need new births in the life and ministry of congregations.

5. Adaptations by institutions, appearance of new institutions, reprioritizing by United Methodism of perceived needs for service—any of these factors alone would provoke special attention to the question of the relationships of the church and non-parish institutions. Since all will be occurring, it is certain that United Methodism will face a recurring, if not constant, call to address the needs of non-parish institutions and the issues of the relationship of those institutions to the church.

The consequences of these five realities can best be seen in terms of their impact on some of the institutional types surveyed for this study. The trends related to hospitals, retirement residences, and children- and youth-serving agencies all point to greatly increased outreach and prevention activities. These trends reflect two developments: (1) the discovery that primary responsibility of health, including mental health, rests with the individual and his or her family (and perhaps friends); (2) the growing ability of senior citizens to maintain their own homes for many years after retirement. Each development leads to perceptions of growing need for supportive services. Such services could help individuals build knowledge and skill in caring for themselves, or they may provide certain aspects of care that the individual cannot do very well for him- or herself.

The outreach programs found in several of the health and welfare institutions surveyed are responding to this reality. In addition, community centers are sometimes involved through the community organizations with which they work in attempting to get the health-care system to provide accessible and relevant services in their community. Even some colleges are finding growing student interest in learning health-enhancing recreational activities that can be pursued after college.

In all these ways, non-parish institutions are adapting to the situation. However, the need for community-based health-support activities is not limited to neighborhoods in which a community center is located. Futhermore, most congregations can be involved in helping their own constituents to meet such needs, particularly in terms of health education and outreach to the elderly. In some communities, churches will surely be cooperating in such health-care programs as "Wholistic Health Centers," church-based health programs that include ministers and health professionals on the basic treatment team. When that happens, there is a strong possibility that a new non-parish institution will eventually be formed to manage this service.

In short, this one set of changing needs will be (and to some degree already is) entailing adaptations in program in many types of institutions, eliciting new programming in local churches, and calling forth newly created non-parish institutions. Because of these consequences, there will be a need for United Methodism to coordinate local-church programming with institutions, to consider relating to new institutions, to amend its expectations to meet the adaptations of its already existing related institutions, and to find ways to facilitate connections between agencies that normally do not relate much with one another and are connected with different bodies in conference or national board structures of the church. And all those consequences arise from just one sequence of probable changes that is only one aspect of the basic trends noted in chapter 4.

College developments provide a further illustration of what we know is in store, because it is already starting to happen. The growth of various public funding programs for students in private colleges coupled with a decline in the usual college age group raises the priority of student recruitment for all colleges and universities. Almost certainly, United Methodist-related colleges will be trying to utilize their church connection more effectively for recruitment. This will not be simply a matter of seeking referral of member youth as students. Contacts will be sought with church members who have access to broader ranges of student recruitment. For instance, a college may want to convince United Methodists who are high school guidance counselors to be sure information on the college and some encouragement to consider it is presented to all students in the school who might potentially be interested in enrolling at the college.

Another example of the ripple effect of small changes is the trend among colleges to try to broaden the geographical base from which they are able to attract students—an obvious step to counter the decreasing pool of potential students in any one area. This step will have the consequences of increasing the competition among United Methodist colleges, but that need not be bad. For instance, in order to compete in another college's traditional territory, a school will have to surrender some sense of "our turf" in their own region to others. Broadening the geographical base will have the additional consequence of giving a better opportunity for survival to the colleges that can do the best job of attracting students. Those colleges with quality programming and effective management will thus have a better chance to survive the crunch of the 1980s. This fact, in turn, will provide a relatively objective means of screening just which schools are most able to attract students and who are thus best able to discharge their primary mission. Also, the college surrendering turf rights will probably experience some easing of pressures to conform to one or another person's image of what a United Methodist college ought to be, since there will be more options available for those who want something different than the local college has to offer.

Some institutions of each type surveyed, except colleges, indicated involvement with advocacy activities. As the nation gropes to find its way into some suitable form of universal health coverage, and as welfare needs are assumed to be the duty of the government, concern for the needs of persons will increasingly involve outreach into the political arena. For instance, retirement homes and community centers will surely be joining with local-church and conference representatives in many states to lobby for effective and appropriate standards for nursing homes, residences, and boarding homes. Similarly, children- and youth-serving agencies will be joining with other social action groups to work on the issue of battered or sexually abused children. General education of the public will be a part of that campaign, but it will surely include political lobbying as well. Hospitals may want to join with these agencies, community centers, and church groups to press for appropriate public health measures. To do so will necessitate moving into such controversial areas as occupational safety and health, environmental regulation to reduce air, water, and land pollution, and no-smoking regulations. Thus, the coming years may see other non-parish institutions as well as community centers involved in controversy (and the potential of some public relations difficulties with some United Methodists as a result).

Given their record of adaptation to meet changing needs and the signs of threats to survival being reported by several types of agencies, institutions will be strongly tempted to fall into a survival syndrome that lets anxiety about survival take priority over openness to emerging needs. The focus of the institution subtly shifts from outreaching concern to anxious grasping. Just as a congregation can destroy its capacity to attract new members by its anxiety over needing members, so an institution that falls into the survival syndrome is in double jeopardy. It might manage to survive while losing sight of what was worth saving, becoming a social "body without a soul."

More likely it will not survive, at least not in its present form. Given the social trends now operating, it is unlikely that institutions that lose sight of their special purpose can long attract support and participation. With so many institutions of so many kinds competing for attention, people will tend to respond to those which most clearly fulfill their values or meet their needs.

In short, each institution will need to be clear about its mission. The term is used here in the secular sense of what does the agency exist to do and for whom? Mission statements have become a common part of business practice, in large measure because of the issues outlined here. If a unit does not know why it is in business, it has no baseline against which to measure the wisdom of its decisions. Similarly, United Methodist-related institutions need to be sure why they are "in business." Furthermore, the answer to that question is also their answer to questions on the mission the agency performs on behalf of The United Methodist Church.

As these examples show, what we can expect next is continuing change, continuing challenge to our assumptions about mission and about relations to non-parish institutions, and constantly renewed opportunities for service. The issue that will be before church and institution will be how to respond.

CHAPTER 8

Where Do We Go from Here?

Where we go from here will be worked out individually by each unit of United Methodism with the institutions with which it relates. This study cannot offer prescriptions for any one of those dialogues. However, eight steps United Methodism can take are identifiable. They can serve as a stimulus and guide for discussions within local churches, Annual Conferences, national boards, and other United Methodist agencies. They may also serve as a useful checklist in discussions with institutions to plan their future United Methodist relationships. We will discuss each one briefly, but let us first get the whole list before us:

1) Recognize that persons' needs, not institutional needs, deserve primary United Methodist concern.
2) Identify clearly which United Methodist bodies are in relationship with which institutions.
3) Clarify mutual expectations with each institution.
4) Provide an ongoing severance option for institutions.
5) Develop effective procedures for each function that should connect an institution and the church.
6) Encourage adaptation to changing needs and opportunities.
7) Be open to new institutions.
8) Emphasize resourcing of local churches and community groups by the institutions.

Keep Person-Needs Primary

Logically, this point is simply restating what we have learned about the history and operation of institutions. Their justification for being, their mission on behalf of United Methodism, is their service in helping persons to meet needs. Psychologically, however, there are three consequences of this basic affirmation, and they are not at all easy to apply consistently.

First, all the institutions studied (and virtually all the rest of the vast array for whom those studied were just a sample) are fundamentally engaged in a healing ministry. They are descendants of Jesus' charge to his disciples to heal the sick, to cast out demons. As such, their proclamation of good news to the poor, the sick, and oppressed is a proclamation in action rather than in words. We need to remember that Jesus rarely combined a command for discipleship without healing outreach; the evangelistic quality of his healing was in the authenticity of the act. Conversely, without those demonstrations of good news in action, the verbal proclamation becomes hollow.

Being ready with the word of evangelism is the task of the congregation (including those of its members who are the administration and staff of related institutions). The institution proclaims by act. If needs are genuinely met and if the relationship between church and institution is close enough on mutual understanding and values, the proclamation will be authentic. Then the church will have the opportunity to respond with the word of gospel whenever an institution's actions provoke someone to ask, "Now why did you do that?"

Second, the pressures that will come to United Methodist sources for help will more probably come from institutions than from the individuals they serve. There will be a constant temptation to consider actions in terms of what the institution needs. However, the appropriate criteria for decision-making deal with the ends and persons served and with the quality of service provided. The crucial questions are:

Who are the persons who are being served, or will be served?

What needs of theirs will be met through the institution (or through its proposed program)?

Where do the needs of those persons fit in the priority of the United Methodist body for its mission outreach?

How well does it seem the institution will be able to meet the needs?

Is that sufficiently effective?

How much will it cost in time and energy as well as dollars to relate to and be involved with that service?

Do we think that cost is justified by the level of benefits that will be produced?

Third, if it is the needs of persons that are primary, then the critical issue for United Methodist mission is that those needs be met. It is not so important that they be met by an endeavor bearing a United Methodist label. In other words, a case cannot be made that a church-related agency in mission will automatically meet certain needs better than a private or public secular agency. In a mature field of service with many institutions operating, usually within a web of regulations and standards, an ecumenical agency or one related to another denomination or a secular agency may be able to pass the test of the questions listed above. In fact, many United Methodist churches have worked diligently to support community institutions they saw as beneficial and necessary even though those institutions were not United Methodist. Therefore, United Methodists should not take the "United Methodist-related" label as proof that a good job is being done in mission. Each institution can be expected to document its performance in meeting needs, and it is appropriate to compare its performance with the record of other agencies seeking to meet the same needs within the same context.

Of course, there are some potential public relations and image-building gains for United Methodism in being connected with an effective agency. However, such a consideration can legitimately arise only if "all things are equal" in the process of meeting needs. In the first place, as we just noted, people's needs take priority—beginning with the very impetus to serve that gave rise to the institution and the relationship in the first place. Furthermore, being connected with an agency that is less effective than others around it may be image-building, but it is bad public relations because the image built is negative.

Identify United Methodist Related Bodies

The United Methodist bodies should be identified for each related institution. That identification ought to include the name of the church unit (and its place within or beside other units if the name does not make that obvious), as well as the name and address of the person primarily responsible for representing that unit in relationship to the specific institution. In addition, some indication of the history and nature of the relationship would be helpful. How long have this unit and this institution been in relationship? How have they been conducting it, i.e., what contributions are made to one another, what reports are made—by whom and to whom—what issues have been faced, and how have they been resolved?

For any institution where there is more than one United Methodist body in relationship, the identification should include as much definition as possible of the particular roles each relating body plays with the institution. Such data can probably be found by comparing the answers of the different relaters to the question of how they have been conducting their relationship with the institution. It would be useful to identify which of the United Methodist relaters is primary; that is, which one forms the connection for the basic channel of relationship. If their roles are not clear from the data, a special consultation of representatives of the various relating bodies and of the institution may be able to make a determination.

Also, with more than one relater, each of them and the

institution will be better able to fulfill their partnership if it is clear how the various United Methodist groups interrelate with one another. In part this question can be answered by reference to organizational charts. Where two units are in formal organizational contact only by their common amenability to an overarching body, perhaps that body should be informed that it is indirectly related to an institution and has some responsibility for clarifying how the groups that relate to the institution should interrelate to each other. In fact, it would probably be best to proceed by having the various relaters discuss the situation together and work out an answer (which may then be presented to the higher body for authorization).

Without clarifying such information it will be very difficult to take any further steps in working out the terms of relationship or even to make a decision to disaffiliate and sever relationship cleanly and humanely. It may not be necessary to work out all the bureaucratic intricacies, but each relater should know who the other relaters are, how they relate with one another, and how each of them relates to the institution. The common knowledge could provide a foundation for working out shared decisions, and it will at least let each one know the other units that might be affected by its decisions and by whose decisions it might be affected.

Clarify Mutual Expectation

In order to build an effective partnership relationship, or even to test whether one is possible, it will be necessary for the United Methodist relating bodies to work out with each institution their mutual expectations. The church will need a clear understanding with the institution of its mission on behalf of United Methodism. That understanding should focus on the basic purposes of the agency, realizing that its primary function for the church is to meet human need. This understanding should specify:

○ who the persons are (condition, social group, neighborhood, etc.) who are served by the institution;

- ○ what needs of theirs the agency is trying to meet;
- ○ what basic methods and style the institution uses to meet those needs;
- ○ any special features in that approach that reflect church values and concerns; and
- ○ expected developments for the future.

On the basis of these understandings the church unit can determine whether a relationship with this institution is an appropriate expression of United Methodist mission commitments.

Other aspects of United Methodist expectations would have to be agreed on with the institution.

- ○ Regular times and methods of reporting will be needed.
- ○ Agreed minimum results for which the institution will be responsible will permit helpful evaluation that gives guidance to both institution and church for future planning and for their relationship.
- ○ Any special services that are to be offered by the institution to United Methodist constituencies should be clarified, along with the communication channels that will be used in making them available or in negotiating their specific use. For instance, opportunities for volunteer service should be noted, along with the means by which these will be communicated to churches, the processes by which volunteers will be supervised, and the reports that will be made on such involvement (e.g., how often, to whom, how detailed). Similarly, special education programs or consultation services the institution can offer to churches or other United Methodist groups should be noted and agreed on along with the terms on which they can be provided and the procedures necessary to contract for them.

For national board units with networks of institutions (and any conferences with similar networks), it will also be necessary to be clear about the terms involved for participation in the network. This process is already quite clear for those networks in which membership is voluntary, for instance, the Certification Council of the Health and Welfare Division. Other network arrangements will also require agreements on what is entailed in membership—both benefits and obligations. Once the terms are clear, then the church will need to know what the institution plans to do, and they will together need to agree on the ways in which the institution will be held accountable for fulfilling its promises.

Since these suggestions concerning United Methodist expectations apply points discussed earlier in this book, they have been quickly summarized. In addition, clarifying expectations for relationship will involve what the institution expects from The United Methodist Church. Of course, those expectations will vary from one institution to another, depending on their specific situation and their history in relationship with United Methodism; and the church unit need not automatically accept all expectations that are suggested. However, some clues on what might arise were revealed by the interviews in our survey. They can be listed in summary by type of institution surfacing the concern.

Children- and Youth-Serving Agencies:
  o More expression of concern for and involvement with the issues of youth, children, and families by the church.
  o Help people to recognize that even in an age of deinstitutionalization, there is a critical need for institutions such as these for people with severe problems.
  o "Do less better;" that is, when using United Methodist money and energy to support mission, put more effort into selection and concentrate resources to support relatively few efforts at a level that makes a real difference rather than spreading around many small tokens.

Colleges:
  o Help in recruiting students.
  o Help members to understand the mission of higher education, along with its special character and problems.

- ○ Offer, especially through national agencies, technical assistance to help colleges solve problems they face.
- ○ Give moral support for and apply influence on behalf of a value-centered approach to higher education.
- ○ Provide funds or access to funds for special needs and opportunities and/or provide financial aid through scholarships (etc.) for students rather than grants for institutions.
- ○ When choosing trustees for colleges, name persons who are knowledgeable about higher education and who have connections to help with student recruitment and/or fund-raising.
- ○ Supply information on opportunities for work, study, and service that would be meaningful sabbatical experiences for faculty.

Community Centers:
- ○ Provide flexible funding; especially provide seed money for higher risk projects of mission significance that because of their risk would be difficult to fund through secular channels.
- ○ Use more stringent criteria of effectiveness in funding, so that money will be concentrated where it can have the most effect.
- ○ Keep up pressure for self-support, while recognizing that provision of a smaller contribution base means "fewer strings."
- ○ Provide technical assistance through consulting, training, etc.
- ○ Use the church's access to the media to interpret the work of the institutions.
- ○ Stay close to what the agencies are doing, providing moral support and testing their plan of mission against church values, concerns, and priorities, all the while learning what can be used to educate United Methodists on issues.
- ○ Provide one point of "plug in" to United Methodism which would provide full coordination of all its available resources, both local and national.

Hospitals:
- ○ Concentrate on developing other aspects of health care, using hospitals as a base of supportive expertise.
- ○ Help church members to become directly involved with their institutions, so there will be better understanding.
- ○ Try to identify and refer United Methodist health professionals who might be willing to relocate to institutions needing them, particularly those in rural or inner city situations.

Retirement Residences:
- ○ Sustain and strengthen the networks of cooperation, technical assistance, etc. which the Health and Welfare Division provides.
- ○ Help church members to understand better the purpose and functions of retirement residences.
- ○ Build closer relationships between churches and residences.
- ○ Emphasize standard-setting for long-term care, working cooperatively with the institutions to advocate good standards regulated by state and local agencies.

Miscellaneous Mission Agencies:
- ○ Take a personal interest in institutions, encouraging United Methodists to seek ways to work with them in vocation or through volunteering.
- ○ Be flexible in relating to different agencies, varying the "rules" in order to treat all fairly.
- ○ Help agencies to do effective needs assessments.
- ○ Learn from the institutions' experiences and successful innovations to build programming in local churches.

When the church and the institution lay out their expectations, each will have the opportunity to determine which ones they will be able to meet. When these responses are shared, it will be possible to work out mutually agreeable expectations which each partner is willing to meet. With that clear it will be possible for both the church body and the institution to decide whether the benefits of the relationship for them are sufficient to justify the "costs" involved in meeting the finally agreed on expectations. If the decision is favorable, this process of clarification will have laid the foundation for an effective partnership in mission. When it is not, there will be a clear basis on which to consider whether severance of relationship is the best option for both parties.

Include a Severance Option

Although the history and tradition of most relationships between United Methodism and its institutions have a "family" quality to them, the more accurate image of cooperation for common mission goals is that of a business partnership. That is, the partners agree to the relationship because they see benefits for themselves that outweigh the costs and because they affirm the purpose of the connection. Naturally, if either partner decides that the other is not living up to their agreements or if either decides that the purposes are no longer essential to them or that the costs have begun to overshadow the gains, then it is time to consider restructuring the relationship or ending it altogether.

For those reasons, one aspect of every agreement to maintain relationship should be an "out" clause. Such a clause can take either one of two forms. Either partner may have the right to withdraw from relationship upon notification of the other. Alternatively, each could covenant with the other not to withdraw until there was an opportunity for mutual reconsideration. If the latter option is chosen, there must be a clear procedure to request reconsideration and a time limit for response, after which unilateral withdrawal would be permitted. Obviously, such an agreement does not need to be treated as legally binding (in fact, it would probably be better for it not to be so rigid). However, it would have moral force for each party and would provide a way for their concerns about continuance or discontinuance to be channeled. The key point of such a clause is assurance to the partners that if conditions change, they have a way out.

In fact, it would be desirable to match the "out" clause with a "sunset" clause. The latter would set a time limit on the relationship agreement and mandate that it be reviewed and renewed before that limit or it will automatically expire. Two approaches to such a limit are possible. One sets a term of years (e.g., five or ten), with a specific date of expiration. The other mandates review when there are relevant changes in either party and sets a target date for review a limited time after a change occurs. One such change would be the coming of a new chief executive officer to the institution. The corresponding change for United Methodist bodies might be the quadrennial election of a new board, although that less clearly means a significant change in conditions. Such a clause would require, for instance, that the agreement would expire unless reviewed and renewed within one year after a new administrator takes office.

Putting those two clauses together, each party is assured of opportunities to reconsider the relationship and the right to seek termination. The "sunset" clause guarantees periodic review. The "out" clause guarantees a process of review whenever either party becomes dissatisfied with the arrangement. Perhaps those clauses ought also to provide for a way of calling all other United Methodist bodies that relate with the institution into the review.

Develop Functions that Connect Institution and Church

One of the difficulties in relationships which our study showed was that they can often hang "in the air," leading to further distance between institution and church and to a smaller and smaller proportion of United Methodists knowing anything about the institution and very possibly being unaware of its relation to United Methodism, or even of its existence. To prevent that situation it will be necessary for the partners in relationship to develop specific procedures to make operative the key functions they agree should exist in the relationship. If such procedures cannot be developed to the mutual satisfaction of both parties, it is probable that the relationship is really just a token one. If so, it will need to be redefined or terminated. Any relationship that is sustained as a token tends to weaken the "currency" of relationship and thus undercuts others that are potentially much stronger. Some examples of what could be done will indicate what is involved in this step to sound relationship.

Colleges have indicated that help in recruiting students is important to them. If an Annual Conference agrees that it will cooperate in helping to encourage United Methodist high school seniors to consider attending a United Methodist-related school, specific means will have to be designed and implemented for this to occur or it will be an empty agreement. Our survey suggests that it would be better to approach the recruiting task from a broad base, involving more schools than just one, so that the church is able to offer meaningful choices to its youth and avoid the unfortunate stance of "selling them" on a particular school.

For instance, a simple information packet on the school or schools should be available for pastors to use with youth (and perhaps adults considering a return to school). Concrete advice should be included on how to use the information and how to share it with high school counselors to secure the cooperation of the high school. Since pastors will need to use the material if the process is to work, an Annual Conference will need to plan to encourage that use. For instance, it could ask for the number of young people referred to United Methodist colleges as a part of the pastor's annual report to conference. The conference could also join with the college(s) to cosponsor an annual seminar at the school for pastors. That seminar would be an opportunity for pastors to become better acquainted with the school and learn to use the packet. However, not many would attend unless the seminar also included opportunities for their own continuing education and/or a chance to enter into dialogue with representatives of the college on the value issues of young adults (perhaps comparing the perspectives of college and local church pastor).

Several types of institutions asked for a personalizing of their relationship with local churches, and many churches have learned through contacts with missionaries as well as contacts with non-parish institutions that the benefits for a supporting congregation go up markedly when there is a personal point of interest and source of information. If a conference and one or more of its related institutions want to use this personalizing function to make their relationships stronger, several steps could be taken. One of the most important would be to encourage local churches to become specific partners with an institution or one of its programs. Staff and participants of the agency could then be included in the prayer life of the church and its members. Personal letters to and from individual staff members or participants could provide a personal dimension. Obviously the number of churches that can relate that closely with any one institutional unit will be limited; communicating with United Methodists is a byproduct of mission, first priority must go to the basic work of the agency. Nevertheless, a conference could organize the program among churches if the institution were willing to organize its own participation. If neither is willing to do so, they should admit that they do not really want to personalize the relationship as much as they want to contain the amount of effort that must be spent on it.

Still another possible form of connection relates to the request of several types of institutions for more workers who are committed United Methodists. In fact, what is needed is a new kind of missionary, though not working under that name; therefore, a new system of missionary recruitment is needed. If institutions and national boards were to cooperate, conferences and local churches could take an active part in making such a process a reality.

The institutions would need to supply data on personnel needs, not just to fill immediate vacancies, but also those that frequently recur. The boards would need to assemble, analyze, and package these data so that they would be useful, for instance, in counseling with adults who are determining where to invest their career or are considering a mid-life career change, or in discussions with high school and college youth trying to decide on their vocational commitments. The boards could disseminate the material through conferences, who could in turn put it into the hands of the local churches that would most likely be able to use it. It would be most productive if the general material were backed up by a telephone information system that made data available on specific needs. The local church could then use the material with its own people, through counseling by the pastor and through programs for youth. A later benefit for the church recruiting such a "missionary" will be the potential ongoing personal contact with the institutions in which he or she serves.

A final example of what connection means relates to hospitals, the institutional type in our study which consistently showed least closeness to United Methodism and most often suggested church concentration on needs in its field other than its own institutional support. One potential point of partnership often mentioned by hospital personnel was providing data and expert resources for local-church and other United Methodist bodies to deal with the personal, family, and community base for health. A cooperating conference and hospital would need to find ways to bring hospital leaders and local church people into dialogue on issues and possibilities.

An alternative approach would be for the Health and Welfare Ministries Division to take the lead in conjunction with the network of hospital administrators. By consulting with panels of church leaders (e.g., General Council on Ministries, the Board of Church and Society, and the Board of Global Ministries), a number of critical points of common concern could be identified. Each of these could become a churchwide theme for a year or longer, during which a special study could produce some clear models for thought and action on the issue. These models could then be the basis for a series of regional conferences that would bring together people from several hospitals and conferences, from United Methodist Women, and probably from a variety of other interested non-parish institutions. These regional conferences would equip their participants to stimulate similar discussions among concerned United Methodists and institution representatives in each community with a related hospital.

One possible theme might be the elderly and their self-care. It would tap a major concern of many local churches, retirement residences, and community centers as well as hospitals. A team of two representatives from each system could spend a week in Edinburgh, Scotland, studying the system of conjugate housing and mutual care that provides effective, close support for the self-care of older persons there. Those representatives could then design an adaptation of that model to the American scene and The United Methodist Church. The regional workshops and perhaps a study unit with workbook could be the outcome of the process, leading in turn to work with local churches and finally to greater cooperation among institutions and churches and to more effective ministry to the needs of older Americans.

Encourage Adaptation

Since the United Methodist commitment to the work of non-parish institutions is based on concern that persons' needs are met, the traditional institutional stance of adaptation to changing needs should be affirmed and encouraged. Two implications of that stance can be noted. First, while the institutions have a history of adaptation, the built-in danger for any institution is to become fixated in their way of looking at problems and organizing themselves to solve those problems. Consequently, they may not see signs that point in a different direction than their orientation, or they may have a very hard time shifting priorities and staff capacities to meet the change. Probably this danger increases with the size and specialized complexity of the institution (our survey raised the suspicion that colleges may be the most likely to suffer from it at present). Therefore, the church should keep its influence consistently on the side of the institution's openness to new opportunities and to changing conditions that may limit the effectiveness of its present operation.

Secondly, however, as church units relate to institutions, they tend to focus their relationship on certain channels and often specify the use of funds. This tendency carries the weakness of seeing too little to be able to encourage adaptation. It also could lead to some bureaucratic rigidity within the system of United Methodist relaters that subtly encourages the institution not to change in order to avoid the necessity of adapting the church's means of relating to the institution. Thus, the institution needs always to use its influence to help the United Methodist bodies with which it relates to be open to new possibilities, both those the institution sees and those United Methodists may see in other parts of their ministry which could be potentially important to the institution.

Consider New Institutions

It is certain that every year some United Methodists somewhere will have an opportunity to start a new non-parish institution. New forms of needs will surely be discovered, and our history shows we tend to respond to them in many cases by creating an institution to care for them. As long as the church wants to minister to persons in need, its stance must be one of openness to new needs and to new ways of ministering to them. On the other hand, it is appropriate to learn from experience that the early days of institution formation are the most demanding on the church's time and money. Thus, if there is any way the need can be met through existing institutions, local churches, other channels of United Methodist activity, or through cooperation with other agencies (religious or secular, public or private), those alternatives probably should be preferred.

There are essentially three questions that must be answered

in the affirmative before a new institution should be developed to respond to a need. (1) Are the needs we see really important ones? Does it reflect basic United Methodist commitments to respond to them? (2) Will it be beyond the capacity of existing agencies, churches, etc. to sustain response to this need, or will it cause serious disruption for them to try to adapt or add programs as might be required to meet the new need? (3) Will new resources to enable response be unlocked by the creation of a specific agency?

Only when these points are clear should a new institution be started. Since it is likely that many situations across the country will call for that action, two special criteria should be borne in mind from the beginning, based on the data found in our survey. First, the institution should be planned to keep overhead needs as low as possible. For instance, physical facilities and office support could be shared with other agencies or churches. Until the agency is well established it should avoid commitments to purchase or build property. Instead, space may be leased or "borrowed"—through the contribution of a church or other agency.

Second, the program or programs being shaped into an institution should be able to demonstrate a clear potential for generating self-support, whether from revenues produced by its operations or by use of standard community and/or government funding support mechanisms. Startup grants from church, foundation, or other sources will not be sufficient. Though they are often necessary to bridge the period from the beginning of the agency until it achieves self-support, this cannot usually be a very long period. "Seed money" is usually given for only a very few years (e.g., two, three, or maybe five) and usually with decreasing amounts over the term to phase-in self-support. However, an institution implies activity over a long term. Making that term feasible will require that the work of the agency produce revenue. Thus, United Methodism will need to be prepared to see its new institutions in a more independent form of partnership almost from the beginning. Keeping them close and dependent will undercut the capacity for self-support.

Emphasize Resourcing

One clear trend for the future is that many needs which may have seemed successfully delegated to institutions long ago are returning to the doorstep of the local church. As we have seen, care of the elderly, support for families, training for parenting, assistance for economic development, and support for health self-care are all becoming active potentials for a congregation's ministry with its members and community. Also, many more such claims on caring in the congregation are undoubtedly developing. Accordingly, one important aspect of the church/institution relationship should focus on assistance by institutions in providing resources for local churches to use in responding to such opportunities. Three forms of resource will be needed.

1. Information on needs and possible responses can come from the work and research of the institutions. Also, their experience can be used in mission assessment processing by local churches to identify needs among their members and in the community. That process could also enable the church to use data from the most effective responses of others as standards against which to compare what it is doing to meet needs regarding health, family life, care of the elderly, preparation for aging, community deterioration, etc.

2. Programs local churches can use could include curriculum materials for Christian education programs or special adult or family study groups. Family life, preparation for aging, health self-care, etc. are all good potential subjects for local-church involvement. Other resources might be in terms of methods a congregation could use for programs. For instance, a process could be developed and distributed to recruit and train active older adults to provide personal contact and some other services such as buying, transporta-

tion, or even feeding for other elderly persons less able to be out but still wanting to stay in their own home.

3. Institution staff with special expertise could consult with churches as they build their program to help people be more effective. Some programs may even need an ongoing supervisory relationship, because of the difficulties of maintaining activities effectively. An agency staff group could design a program that could be operated by volunteers with adequate supervision and provide the training, professional supervision, and coordination required. In that way the agency staff would provide service for many more persons than they could with their own institutional programs alone, while the local church would be moving into significant mission. As an added benefit, the process should create more appreciation in the church and the community of the institution and its work.

The key to such resourcing will be the conference units that relates to the institutions. They are in the best position to work with the agency to get cooperation in a venture like this because of their partnership agreement. Through conference channels institutions would also have contact with local churches and the opportunity to identify those that can best model the new form of partnership in mission because of their perceptiveness, aggressive leadership, and closeness to the needs of the community. Once creatively started in this way, a more common conference formal and informal communication process will encourage more churches to try, and the institutions will have an interested constituency to which to respond with resources.

As we end our journey through the wild and wonderful land of relationships to non-parish institutions, let us review the major sights we have seen. Institutions have grown up as expressions of United Methodist concern to meet needs in the community. Meeting those needs is still the primary reason for the existence of the institutions. It is not finally necessary to have an institution that is United Methodist related to meet needs that United Methodism wants met. The future will continue to bring changes and with them new perceptions of needs and opportunities. The time has come to work out clear partnership agreements between United Methodism and its related institutions. In that process, some relationships will probably be terminated and many will need strengthening.

The means to our ends are many and so are our mandates and missions. We must not assume that just because an institution has been around a long time and has been United Methodist related that we should continue the relationship. Neither must we assume that just because an institution's activity does not seem to be very "religious" it does not express United Methodist mission. The only safe assumptions are that God will continue to challenge the church to minister to needs, that special institutions will on some occasions be the best vehicles for doing so, and that any United Methodist unit and institution that wants to be in genuine relationship will have to work to make it productive.